"I don't care if you are the football captain . . . the star . . . the All-American or the third string guard or the fifth-stringer who may never see a minute's action. Be proud . . . for football is the game for a chosen few. Just being a part of it makes you a better man . . . a more loyal man . . . a better citizen."

—John Gagliardi

GAGLIARDI
OF ST. JOHN'S

- The Coach
- The Man
- The Legend

By John Gagliardi and Don Riley

Published by Joel Montpetit and Ralph Turtinen Publishing Co.
240 Minnetonka Avenue South
Wayzata, Minnesota 55391
612/473-3722

Printed in the United States of America
By Foss Printing

I dedicate this book to St. John's University . . . to the hundreds of fine young men who have played for me . . . to my loyal and loving family . . . and to attorney Joel Montpetit, who had enough faith in our work and words to publish this book.

—John Gagliardi

Table of Contents

GAG, THE MAN 10

AN INTERVIEW WITH GAG 13

FOREWORD 17

CHAPTER 1
The Making of a Winning Football Coach ... 21
Play A: A Simple Pass Strikes Fear 26

CHAPTER 2
The Goals of a Winning Coach and Team ... 29
Play B: Bootlegger's Delight 34

CHAPTER 3
The Theory Behind Gag's 'Social' Practices .. 37
Play C: Guards Become Big Play Men 42

CHAPTER 4
Football Means Solving Problems 45
Play D: Right Sweep to Eternity 50

CHAPTER 5
Eyeballing the Prospects 53
Play E: Trickery May Get You Everything ... 58

CHAPTER 6
Foreign Fields, Weather, Fans and Pep Talk . 61
Play F: How to Spring the 'Trap' 66

CHAPTER 7
Coaching Underdogs and Favorites 69
Play G: A Pleasant Embarrassment 74

CHAPTER 8
Deciding on the Nature of the Beast 77
Play H: A Wall of Success 82

CHAPTER 9
Control vs Lightning and Gimmickry 85
Play I: "Mash-Mouth" Football 90

CHAPTER 10
The Theories of Defense 93
Play J: Putting the Kick in the Kickoff Return 98

CHAPTER 11
Anatomy of an Important Victory 101

CHAPTER 12
The St. John's Blocking System 109

(Continued on next page)

Table of Contents (Continued)

CHAPTER 13
Selling Your School 115

CHAPTER 14
The Days of Decision and Turmoil 121

CHAPTER 15
Little Things Count 127

CHAPTER 16
Unlikely Heroes Are St. John's Legacy 133

CHAPTER 17
The Anguish of a Losing Season 139

CHAPTER 18
Reflections on Coaches, Losing and
Other Things 147

POSTSCRIPT 155
What Peggy Gagliardi Says about Gag 157
What Gina Gagliardi Says about Gag........ 159

MORE QUOTES FROM JOHN.................. 161

ABOUT DON RILEY......................... 168

Gag, The Man

Imaginative Italian Blood Makes Changing Easy

He's been known for years as perhaps the most adaptable football coach in America: changing formations, styles, players from position to position and changing battle orders on the eve of key games. Change wears well on a football leader who apparently comes by it through the warm Italian blood which flows through his veins. John Gagliardi explains:

"My father was an Italian immigrant who landed in Trinidad, Colorado, at the age of 16. Like so many Italian immigrants and Slovakian workers in those days, he was familiar with the hard work the mines supplied, so he was a miner. But as work in the mines slowed, my dad proved to be adaptable. He then became a blacksmith. When horses were on their way out and automobiles on their way in, my dad opened a body and paint shop for cars. I loved that man because he never panicked when life styles changed. He flowed right along with them.

"I think he epitomized the old Italian expression, *Casara, serra* — whatever will be will be. He always told me, 'John, don't try to change the world overnight. Live each day fully. The days will take care of themselves.' Today, we'd call it going with the flow. I think the reason I can make moves without razzing myself in football is because I follow my dad's example. I try to shift with the tide. I don't fight it. If we don't have a passer, let's run. If we don't have the runner, let's pass. I come by the changes very easily."

What few people realize is that Gagliardi was perhaps the youngest football coach in grid history. At 16 he captained and coached his Trinidad St. Mary's football team when the coach was called to war. Through the age of 20 he coached St. Mary's to a brilliant 36-6 record and even got to two state Catholic tournaments.

"After graduation I attended Trinidad Junior college and played basketball and took typing and coached St. Mary's. I had the fun of competition on the floor and one night hit 36 points. I had the thrill of coaching youngsters — and I also became the best damn typist in Colorado."

Coming from a large family of nine children, Gagliardi needed help to get to college. A kindly priest in Trinidad was enthralled with Gag's coaching and inspired him to continue his education. At Colorado College John majored in physical education. After graduation, the same priest, upon hearing Carroll College in Helena, Montana, was thinking about giving up football, talked the administrator into letting John coach one year. The price was right: an opening salary of $2,200.

"That sounded like a million dollars — and to get a chance to coach. What luck!" John recalls. "Well, I guess I did something right. Carroll was getting ready to drop football because of the expenses. It was really floundering.

"Well, we turned it around with a 24-6 mark for four years — and it's still going there 35 years later. I'm proud of that. I'm proud, too, that I learned to coach without the aid of many assistants. I usually had one or two. That way, I had to learn about all facets of the game. I had as much fun designing defenses as plays; as much fun learning about my players' personalities as I did about their physical abilities.

"I thank the Lord I learned my football in small schools and colleges where I was given the chance to make mistakes and correct them; where I could be my own man. I don't know if I could have ever forged a decent record had I come up in a big system, just one of 14 or 15 assistants. I was very fortunate."

So we see a Gagliardi who was self-taught.

"That's about it. I benefited from mistakes. I would scratch down plays between typing classes. I worked in my dad's garage and he knew I wasn't much of a body or paint man. But it gave me the chance to think, and I would always be scribbling down notes about football. While I was hammering out a fender, I was thinking about third and one situations.

"Then I'd rush out on the St. Mary's high school field, filled with new ideas. I'd be amazed when one would work and we'd score a touchdown. It was like a scientist making a big break-through against a virus. He couldn't feel more elated."

So it was the perfect blend: typing classes...work in the body shop... basketball for the junior college...and coaching St. Mary's. And my, what coaching John turned in.

He was the baseball coach and the track coach and the basketball coach. Same at Carroll. If they would have had a skiing course, John would have volunteered.

"I learned something from all that coaching; namely that winning doesn't necessarily mean how much you know about the sport. Gosh, I got information out of books and talking to old veterans and listening to the radio. I really wasn't a gifted student of basketball or baseball. But I learned to let the players operate on their own instincts. I learned how to handle young men. That's the greatest asset in coaching — handling the young people. I found that we could win by how I directed their minds rather than the techniques

Gagliardi's confidence grew as his record did. At St. Mary's and Carroll, coaching sometimes as many as four sports a year, he had a remarkable 77 percent victory record. Considering his age and the variety of sports, it stands as perhaps an all-time figure in the realm of coaching records.

"The move to St. John's certainly was not difficult. I got a raise to $4,000 a year. Gosh, almost double my Carroll salary. I left Carroll in good hands. The young priest who took over for me went on to become an archbishop in Seattle.

"But at St. John's I also coached other sports — including hockey. I didn't know a puck from a peach but we had some splendid records."

Splendid indeed — the finest records in St. Johns's hockey history.

"I guess what I'm getting at is that I was very fortunate to get involved in so many sports. I found out that it's attitude more than style. If a team believes, it can win. Believing is everything. Oh, you have to be disciplined and organized — but it's not the knowledge of the sort as much as the knowledge of handling players that win."

Just what are some of the key factors in handling players?

"Never berate a man's abilities. That doesn't mean you can't lecture him or crack the whip; but never tell a youth he doesn't have ability. If you crack down, be sure you explain you are doing it because he has SO MUCH ability you can't stand to see it wasted. If you tell a boy he is worthless, you can destroy him. But if you tell him he is wasting his fine God-given talents, then you are replenishing his will to win. He can become angry at you but not unforgiving. He knows that you want him to win and to fulfill his potential.

"Getting to know the boy is hard work. I am still learning after over 40 years of coaching. I am still trying to get inside heads. At St. John's it sometimes becomes very difficult because we dress so many players and turn none away. I know over the years that I have not gotten to know that many players all that well. I can only hope they forgive me and can understand the problem. In four years I will coach nearly 200 players. If I get to know 50 fairly well, that is about all that a human being can expect. I know some don't get the attention they deserve. That, too, is a problem with a large squad and small staff. But I keep trying and each year try to know more boys well.

"The beautiful thing is the number of Johnnies who write me later on to tell me how much they got out of the program — even if they didn't start or were never that well known to me personally. One fine surgeon wrote me recently that he learned more about life and sharing in four years of St. John's football than he did in four years of medical school. That nearly brought tears to my eyes."

"Trinidad was small enough with about 10,000 people so you knew people well and they supported you. My father and mother were great supports. They encouraged me to go to college and that wasn't easy since I was the first in a large family. I got a work ethic from my dad; nobody works harder than a miner or blacksmith or body shop man. I learned hard work in the body shop. I learned you can go to school and work at avocations with fierce intensity. I learned that work can be fun and fun can be work.

"I was very lucky to arrive at the right family at the right time in the right place. My dad not only worked, but he had the Italian touch of artistry. I think I got some of those genes,too. He wanted his paint jobs to be the best. I want my coaching to be the best. You certainly are a product of your environment. I was a product of love, work, desire and ambition."

John's mother is still alive today but his father has died. One brother went on to play Big 10 football and is coaching today. Another brother still runs the auto repair shop in Trinidad.

"All of my brothers and sisters grew up to know work — but more important, to love their work. I can only tell young coaches in under-staffed schools: don't complain. Get into as many sports as you can. Learn to understand human nature. That's where it's all at — not on the blackboard.

An Interview with Gagliardi

August 1, 1976 — St. Paul Pioneer Press

When the district attorneys aren't chasing down sadistic hockey butchers, Little League mothers are trying to engineer 1981 major league contracts for their tykes. And clubhouse meetings are held in union halls and judges' chambers... As the man pleaded the other day, "My Lord, can't you tell me where sports are fun anymore?" Yah. I could think of one place. Maybe the only haven in the country where they measure talent by wisecracks and puns over first downs; where they issue popsicles at practice in place of grubby moleskins; where they hang images of coaches only on Christmas trees; where the sun still comes up after a loss; where the quarterback still calls his own plays; where the telephone company never got an order to install a pressbox phone; where there isn't a limp at an alumni dinner and where one player always seems to wind up with No. 100 on his jersey...

Pure, unadulterated, dreamy fantasy. No. They call it St. John's University. And between laughs and schmaltz and luck and love it wins 75.5 percent of the time, knocks rivals on their ears and spawned a mentor who has given up moonlighting because coaching is too much fun to share—even with an expanded billfold. Listen, Virginia, and you shall know, how John Gagliardi, perhaps the finest and most innovative mind in all of collegiate football, masterminds this miracle in the cloistered nook of greenery that is Collegeville's acres on the outskirts of St. Cloud.

Listen to why and how he has won 11 state college titles, three bowls and three national titles in 31 years at St. John's, along with another eight crowns at such assorted assignments as St. Mary's High School in Colorado Springs, Carroll College in Montana and a junior college you never heard of. And won them without ever giving a single football scholarship!

What makes the Johnnies run?

GAGLIARDI: "Fun. Spirit. Enthusiasm. I don't really know...By the time we sort out the girls, non-Catholics, mediocre students, non-football players, people who want scholarships and those who have never heard of St. John's, we are talking about only a microscopic number. But out of that few come 150 football candidates this fall. And we'll suit them all up. By the end of the year, 10 or so may drop out. The others will have an experience...I guess we do things a little differently."

How so?

GAGLIARDI: "Well, long ago we got rid of the blocking dummies and the sleds and all the apparatus...We never wear football togs during practice. We have fun. We make up plays and laugh at our mistakes. We work on timing and do calisthenics. If the calisthenics are too tough, we cut them out...I don't believe in football injuries. I'm not all that proud of my titles——but I am damned proud that in the last 12 years we haven't had a knee operation. In 23 years here we haven't had four serious football injuries...Most injuries occur in practice. That's insane. We don't play St. John's in football, so why should Johnnies be killing Johnnies? I think we've disproven the theory you have to knock heads and take bites out of each other to be ready to hit on Saturdays..."

So injuries can be controlled?

GAGLIARDI: "I think so. I think it's an outright disgrace that college footballers be maimed, many times for life. The old knee and hip injuries creep up in the future. Look, if a kid is making $50,000 a year for the Vikings, he assumes an injury risk. But my young men are playing for sheer joy and most of them are working their way through school. They don't deserve to be limping 10 years from now."

You're one of the few coaches who lets the team call its own plays and you don't use an aide upstairs. Why?

GAGLIARDI: "Most of my players go on to become professional people—doctors, lawyers, politicians, educators. Hell, they're smarter than I am. I listen to them...I had a little sub a couple of years back who made some fine suggestions. Now he's heading a department at the University of Missouri. My assistant coach at Carroll is now the archbishop of Seattle. He'll be a Cardinal some day. Don't you think I should listen to people like this? Pressbox aides are fine for the other team. I would rather hear it from my players and see it close hand. Last year I got credit for pulling a beautiful surprise play that won a game. My defensive halfback suggested it...I hope I'm teaching the Johnnies to think for themselves."

Are the kids different today—I mean the new breed?

GAGLIARDI: "Today you've got the tank shirts, bare feet, long hair and big glasses. That's just the instructors...Really, styles change, but the boy doesn't. I see no basic differences today than I did 33 years ago. At that time my high school coach was taken into service and the kids coached themselves. The same thing could happen today. I like the young people. They look different, but the will to win and enjoy life and accomplish never ceases."

Johnnies are known for surprising style changes on the field.

GAGLIARDI: "It all depends on my quarterback. We've had quarterbacks who couldn't pass—so we ran 95 percent of the time. We've had passers and put on aerial circuses. Last year we had an option runner, so we threw out our playbook after four games and improvised. Not even our third team really knew what we were doing...This year it's more option—with a running quarterback. We'll make it up as we go along. Whatever fits him."

Like a little Notre Dame, everyone seems to gun for St. John's. How do you handle the pressure?

GAGLIARDI: "Before every season I have the players make a list of the teams they'd most enjoy beating. Usually it's a team that upset us the year before...We don't aim at traditional rivals. And we don't try to key too high for fast starts. I find that teams that open on an emotional binge usually unravel later on.

Any words of adivce that you instill in young footballers?

GAGLIARDI: "Yes. I preach that the most important thing in life is to find a good, understanding wife. Without one, you have no cornerstone on which to build anything."

Chicago papers a few years ago headlined St. John's as the only school that combined fun and games and education to the perfect degree.

GAGLIARDI: "It was a warm story. Other schools, I'm sure, try too. We've been fortunate in that so many of my former players send their sons here. Last year I was giving the starting lineup and mistakenly called one boy by his dad's name...We must be doing something right if the old players send their sons here. I know a lot of kids are stunned by our lack of heavy practice and fancy equipment. But everything seems to work out on Saturday afternoons."

You once agonized over leaving St. John's when such schools as Notre Dame made overtures. Parseghian called you a great mind, and you sold a lot of insurance on the side. Are you sorry you stayed?

GAGLIARDI: "I've loved all the places I've coached. I was flattered by several offers from larger schools. And I've tried insurance. But a man must find his place and then work whole-heartedly in one direction. My place is St. John's. My profession: coaching. I have no regrets."

Without scholarships, how do you manage?

GAGLIARDI: "We must attract the man who wants to come and play for St. John's. He finds a way, part-time jobs, aid from home, loans. Frankly, I never look into how the young man manages to get here. But for those who want something, they seem to find a way. I'm so proud that over 95 percent of my men get their degrees. This is certainly no football factory."

Typical of the St. John's way is the fact that alumni wanted to buy him an automobile a few years back. But the abbott decided it should come from the school. But before they made the presentation a new abbott was appointed. He was a basketball fan. John never got the car.

But obviously he's got something else: The right way...or as he emphasizes: "The St. John's Way."

Foreword

John Gagliardi . . . the name sounds like it belongs to the Renaissance masters of the arts. He is, in fact, a twentieth century craftsman of the gridiron with a football coaching style and technique every bit as distinctive as Di Vinci's or Raphael's.

His quality may be as lasting, too, and its effect on coaching commandments. He has proven himself already, longevity-wise. In 34 years he has become the second most victorious active coach in American college football ranks with 225 victories. His .748 victory percentage is second also among active grid coaches.

Truly, Gagliardi is a master. His inventiveness, his stunningly simplified procedures and his practice routines bring his football teams under constant scrutiny by the purists and the critics. He has won three national championships at St. John's in Collegeville, Minnesota, with material which is best described as "average." He operates without scholarships, yet over 100 players are carried on the roster for home games. Gagliardi seems to find places for all of them at one time or another — big men, medium men, little men, fast men, slow men. He finds places for the cumbersome and inept and, at the same time, they all blossom. Somewhere along the line the synchronization that is the indelible label of Gagliardi teams is stamped on a group of men who win and win and win, almost relentlessly.

Statistics sometimes have a way of getting in the way of a coach's true value even when they are as imposing as Gagliardi's. For instance, he is most proud of the fact that none of the 1,000 players he has coached has ever sustained a permanent injury. Only two of his players have ever had serious knee operations. Proud, too, is John of the remarkable number of his athletes who have been graduated, close to 100 percent.

Gagliardi is one of the rarities of the coaching fraternity who is not known as a "passing coach" or a "running coach" or a "defensive coach." His genius lies in his ability to manipulate his offense and defense to the skills of his players. He has had passing teams. He has had rock-gut power teams. He has won with stingy defenses and recently had a team which traded touchdowns in spectacular fashion while winning nine straight and losing in a thriller in the national playoffs.

Modestly, John will say: "Coaching doesn't win. Players win. The coach only brings out the talent and desire inside the players. The coach provides the spark, adds to the incentive, supplies the discipline and the battle plan. But the execution is all important, and that is in the hands of the players."

On a crucial third-down play, St. John's 320-pound center Jim Hickey was suddenly switched to quarterback. On the first play he dropped back and threw a 45-yard pass, which was turned into a 70-yard touchdown. Asked about the surprising move after the game, coach John Gagliardi explained, "Nothing unusual. The situation called for a pass play, and he is our best passer."

THE BEAUTIFUL FALL SETTING at St. John's forms a backdrop for Gagliardi's sideline discussion with Dennis Lynch in 1962. Dennis went on to become a priest and serves in Wisconsin.

1
The Making of a Winning Football Coach

The most important thing: rapport with the players. They must believe in you. Strike a warm, mutual relationship. You may not always be sure or even know in which direction you are going, but they must have faith and believe in your leadership. That is paramount: their dedication in your ability to lead.

For instance, a play might not be tactically strong—but the players must believe it is. If I send in a play that is geared for a short gain situation, they must believe that it will make that short gain. If I send in a daring, long-range gamble, they, too, must have complete faith in it. This faith is not built on the strategy—but on the man, the coach himself.

Most players will give the leader the benefit of the doubt—at least for a testing period. That includes a priest, a minister, corporate head or politician—the people give you the chance to prove yourself. But comes the day when your theories and beliefs must prove themselves. The football coach, however, is in a particularly precarious position. Often it comes down to one game. Produce or else.

I have found that one common denominator, or one characteristic, runs through winning coaches: the ability of salesmanship. They believe in what they are doing and they get the other people believing, too. Knute Rockne once wrote a friend that he wasn't sure how good a football coach he was, but he thought he was a whale of a salesman because he was peddling his program to the players, school officials and fans. He saw the value of selling. And that is primarily what football coaching is.

The winning coaches believe in what they are doing and they get the other people around them believing, too. That includes school officials, alumni, assistants and the players. There are thousands of sets and formations and plays, but the winning coach finds his way through the maze. The key is that they believe in their plans and programs and have injected that belief with infectious enthusiasm into their people.

It doesn't really matter the play or formation. It is the belief the coach has instilled in his players that it WILL work. Woody Hayes believed in the ground game, won with it and for decades instilled that belief in the ground game in his Ohio State players. Lavelle Edwards at Brigham Young imparts the same feeling of confidence in his aerial game to his Cougars. Simply, the best coaches are the best salesmen.

I like to think I am primarily a good salesman with a good program. I try to get them to believe that whatever we do is best. We call it the "St. John's way!" I like to sell the idea we are unique.

We try to get the most out of whatever assets we have no matter how limited. The good poker players play the cards they have the best they can. The coach is a poker player. I have to use whatever cards I have to my advantage.

Footballers are not fooled. They know the team speed is limited. They know if they are short on muscle. They know if the passing game lacks receivers.

You can only play with what is dealt. You can't control the cards. You can, however, control the way you play the cards.

I once was trying to sell a team on the fact we would win with quickness. A senior and a law student, Joe Wentzel, chuckled, "John, where are we going to get that speed?"

I looked him straight in the eye. "I didn't say speed. I said 'quickness.' There is a difference. Each of us will get quick—if it's only for a yard or two, Joe, we will win with quickness...even if we are not fast."

He looked me back right in the eye and said, "I see what you mean. The other guys may think we're slow. But we know we'll be quick."

Exactly.

Salesmanship.

Another time I told the team we didn't have enough passing to be nifty but we were going to out-muscle the other side with gouge-and-tear football. A 145-pound halfback approached with the look of a man who would be facing a fire-eating dragon.

"Look coach, you'd better find somebody else to knock down 220-pound linemen in that set-up. I'm no candidate for the suicide team."

I put my arm around his shoulder and told him his small stature made him an ideal blocker for angle shots to the lower legs of big men; that he'd love to hear them grunt when they hit the deck. I eased him into the blocking role for a few plays and he knocked down six or seven huge defenders every game. He actually preferred to block rather than carry the ball late in the season. It was strictly a selling job. He had to be convinced that his small size made him an ideal blocker in certain situations. In one game he wiped out a 270-pound all-conference defender on a play that broke the game open. The defender later was a National League star. Salesmanship. Again it provided the key note.

Let's say you are coaching a team with a size handicap. They're not hypnotized. They are sold on the idea that while they are small they can out-maneuver bigger men. They are sold that their mobility is more important than strength.

I warn young coaches to never go into a season making excuses. If you are too small for heavy combat, gear yourself emotionally and mentally for quick-reactions. Once the team believes, it is amazing what a transformation will take place.

The halfback who has never thrown the ball can become an effective passer for a few plays if he believes. I've always told men in this type of situation that Joe Kapp got to the Super Bowl by throwing the worst looking lame ducks the game has ever seen. It's not the spiral but the accuracy the pass is judged on.

IT'S WAY BACK IN 1943 and John is the captain, center front, of the winning Trinidad Trinity High School basketball champions in Colorado. Notice the victory gleam already being focused on championships.

A SOLEMN-LOOKING GAG is graduated from college.

Sell. Sell. Sell. Never waver in your beliefs. Never doubt yourself.

I once knew a young coach who admitted to me after he got fired for a horrendous season that, if he could do it over again, he'd have made one change. It seemed he suffered several lost man-games due to a miserable string of injuries. Each week he'd announce publically, "Well, we lost another key starter today. I don't know how we'll plug the hole." Consequently, his reserve man entered the game unsteady, unsure and certainly with little confidence.

The coach, in retrospect, would have gotten the substitute aside and said, "Now is the chance. You've got all the ability—and now is your chance. I'm sure you can do as well or better than the man you replace."

That might have worked. It would have been salesmanship of a high quality.

I find so many coaches let their own fears and anxieties creep into the minds of the players that they virtually destroy their own team. Nothing corrodes a football team like self doubts.

This I carefully explain to our teams is not the St. John's way. I tell them that we will be prepared, physically and mentally. I tell them they have the weapons. I tell them I believe we have discovered a few things in the rival that can be exploited. I tell them that we have a reputation for winning; that our "St. John's way" must be the best because it has gotten us there so often.

Sell. Keep selling. Young men want to believe. Never cast a doubt about their ability or the plan. I tell them, "St. John's wins because we never panic, that we never lose sight of our battle plan and that the close, tense struggles usually are ours because the foe knows St. John's way is the winning way. Time is always on our side. The weather conditions are always on our side. The wind and the crowd and the turf and the clock always is working for St. John's"

Work:

"I tell young coaches who think they have to work 80 hours a week that their outlook is wrong: work to live, don't live to work. Oh, I know that for five or six months it's a struggle and wives don't see their men that much. But there is a breaking point. Football can be important without strangling its own."

Of course, we get beat. Of course, we run out of time. Of course, fumbles or interceptions can wipe out the best laid plans. But never do our teams go into a game feeling other than it will be ours after an hour of battle; that somewhere along the way our system will win; that somewhere along the line the other side will have a few moments of self-doubt.

If I were to give a high school coach a few words of advice, it would be: always believe because then your players will always believe. Stay resolute in your plan. Panic only sets in when your players have lost faith in the game plan—and you.

This kind of salesmanship usually resolves itself into a team that doesn't beat itself. It operates purposely and patiently, doing its own thing and waiting for mistakes by the enemy that it can exploit to break open the game.

So if your squad is heavy but slow—sell it on the wisdom that strength is still what football is all about If you have little running but lots of passing, sell the squadron the theory that a hot passing hand can beat any defense ever devised. If kicking and specialty teams is your forte, convince the team that this is the area in which games are won and lost and you know more about it than the other team.

Again, sell. Sell yourself. Then sell the players.

Unlike solid merchandise commodities which may or may not reflect the value of the salesman's pitch, football is where the sales pitch can supply the very intangibles of spirit and emotional internal depth that build the character on which the cornerstone of victory is rooted.

What they say about Gag:

"It's curious. The longer I'm away from football the less I think of John Gagliardi as only a coach but the more I think of him as a superior human being. He is more than my ex-coach; he is my friend. He is an excellent coach, of course, but I see more: I see the man; concerned, willing to help others, interested in your success or your problems after you've left school. He is interested in so many more things than just coaching. His dimensions appear unlimited.

"Mostly, I guess he is interested in his young men and their welfare. That goes far beyond the bounds of merely coaching a team to win. The things you learn on his football teams are things directly attributable to life. He doesn't just prepare you for a game. He prepares you for the future."

Lyle Mathiasen

"I think of Gag, and I think about Monday films. Gosh, talk about excitement. There were a lot of us who hoped we'd play on muddy days so our jersies wouldn't be so identifiable. Gag could cut you to the quick. It was a real hot seat. A bad play could be a 'mortal sin.' Oh, the values those sessions taught us. I learned from Gag never to settle for less. I learned that mediocrity is hell. He is a master of techniques and details, but put to the players simply.

"I learned so many lessons. Perhaps the one that stays in my mind is the time I broke my hand in a game in Duluth and didn't tell anyone. But it pained me so much I couldn't put it on the ground. Consequently, we were penalized in a vital touchdown situation and it cost us a score; all because I wanted to be an injured hero. I learned that by being a selfish hero you can destroy those around you. Gag never gave me a bad time. But it's the kind of thing you remember when you play for the man."

Ed Donatelle

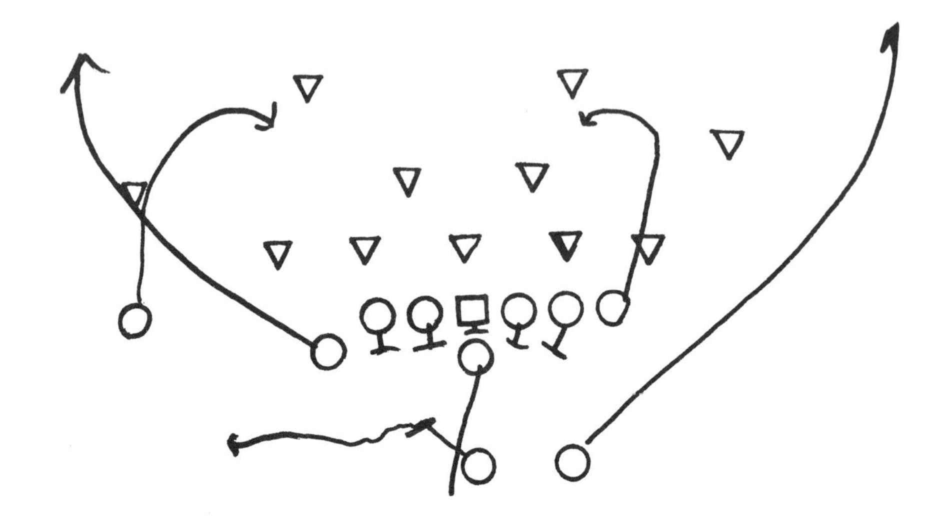

A Simple Pass Strikes Fear

I just call it a "simple" pass but the beauty is presented by the many options. I've always felt a pass play is only as good as what it can provide the passer once original drawing board plans go astray.

This is a play that I figure has won a dozen major title and playoff game victories for St. John's in the last 34 years. It has bailed us out of jams consistently. It is a play that can revitalize a struggling quarterback.

As you see, the quarterback drops back directly from center. He will first ascertain what kind of coverage the strong safety is giving us. The receivers at the same time are hacking out their pass patterns to see what kind of coverage they are getting.

Two of my many fine receivers, Dave Arnold and John Hanowski, were the masters at getting open from the wide receiver spot. Quarterbacks like Dennis Schleper, with his strong arm, and Jeff Norman and John Gagliardi Jr. were gifted at taking whatever the defense would give us. Neither had strong arms, but were excellent at getting what gain they could on what the defense presented.

On this play, Norman used running back Tim Schmitz often as an outlet valve, to unload the ball to the rugged fullback if the deep receivers had problems. And, oh, how the action would erupt when Schmitz would get the ball. Clear the decks for action! He must have averaged 15-18 yards per gain taking the ball near the line of scrimmage. He had power to burn and scored on this very play, carrying us to our third national championship against capable Towson State. This is the same play, with Jim Roeder receiving, that carried us down to the three-yard line with time running out. From here, Norman kicked the winning field goal, virtually as the gun went off.

Big but smooth Mike Grant was excellent at finding openings in any knd of defense from his tight end position. He is the son of the famous Minnesota Viking professional coach and he played with the same cool, confident manner that his father stresses on the NFL sidelines. Grant had amazingly sure hands and today is coaching high school football.

The running back comes up with the big play every few games off this pass. For some reason over the years, the defenses seem to lose track of fast running backs coming out of the backfield. Two who were artists at sifting through into the openings were Marty Cella and Pat Pederson. They were players you must pray to get the ball to in an open field.

That is a play that is excellent for use in high schools because of its simple, yet varied striking power.

Something else. The quarterback, if rushed too badly or harrassed from various angles, can always elect to run off this play—giving us another option. I recall the brilliant ability of Mike Kozlak and Gary Marlow to scramble when no openings were downfield. They sometimes would average six and seven yards carrying the ball when this pass fail didn't materialize.

In other words, this pass play is simply constructed so that there is rarely a primary target. It can be any of four receivers. It can be long or short. It is a play the quarterback loves because of the options. He just does what comes naturally.

This is an excellent first down play when you have a defense staggering. I used it a lot on first downs to keep a strong Gustavus Adolphus team off balance one day. Another time we completed six out of nine from this formation in the last 10 minutes to beat a splendid St. Thomas outfit.

It is simple pass for all occasions. By that I mean it has depth and scope but can be utilized for getting the ball into the hands of tough running backs at top speed.

It goes back to the St. John's tradition for simplicity in all forms of attack. We may look, at times, as if we have a bewildering variety of plays. But believe me we just used various sets to cover the purest of attack fundamentals.

FAMED FOOTBALL LEGEND JOHNNY BLOOD McNALLY, a former St. John's coach, congratulates Gag after a 1982 victory. McNally was a professional great and former professor, who also coached the Pittsburgh Steelers.

2
The Goals of a Winning Coach and Team

Goals. Sometimes a well-meaning but devious issue. We tell our teams that the goal of the other team is to beat St. John's. We tell our players our goal is always the same: a national championship. We set out, I tell our forces, striving for national recognition. We don't think in terms of 6-3 and 7-2 seasons. That's not good enough. I have always set out to win all games and not be content with pin-pointing a few traditional rivals. We strive to win them all.

How do you set about establishing this goal? Well, we tell our players that frankly, the opposition probably will start practice earlier; that they will work harder in practice than us. Then I tell them the all-important basic behind St. John's football: we will work smarter.

Some days I tell my players that the other team this moment is working and straining longer hours, in tougher contact drills, and is risking injury in all out gung-ho, nose-to-nose warfare. But we are thinking, polishing, honing. While they are pitting muscle against muscle, we're putting brain power against brain power. I like to believe—and over the years it has proven out—that at the end of the season our foes are becoming tired physically, which transforms itself into tired thinking. They will be accumulating bruises and ills and we will, hopefully, have accumulated mental toughness, garnished with quick reactions and ability to "read" the game.

There are those who will argue vehemently that mastery over the game accrues only in pressurized practice. I only know that over the years my teams have continued to play fresh football down through the stretch. While other teams have piled up injuries we, fortunately, have piled up point totals. I have found us to be solid finishers from the middle of the season on, when the attrition of injuries and the assorted bumps take their toll of other teams. I think you will find our victory percentage in the last half of the season 25 percent higher than in the first half. I attribute that to fresh bodies and intelligent dispensation of emotion.

In other words, the rivals have worked much harder during the year, but we competed with them favorably in the physical phase of the game and out-steadied them emotionally and showed more character under duress.

So our goal is easily stated: we are not trying to kill the opposition—only score more points and aiming at healthy bodies playing intelligent football and capturing national prestige. In short, we set as our ultimate aim a happy squad winning games.

OK, so you say that sounds so simple. Quite the contrary. A major college coach and I were once discussing this concept and he said to me, "I want to be more realistic, John. I look at our schedule and say, we should win six games and we might get lucky and win seven. There are always three teams I feel we simply can't play on even terms. I tell our squad that they should be proud of winning seven games in a 10-game schedule against top flight opposition."

I don't buy that. I believe we can win every game we play—and that means even if suddenly the Chicago Bears loom on the horizon.

I believe that football has so many varied aspects that based on 22 men against 22 anything is possible. I believe that the other team may have as much advantage as having 14 or 22 players individually superior but that a unified, thinking, believing foe can still win. The 60 minutes and 130-140 plays offer so many opportunities on defense and offense that an inferior team personnel-wise can beat a superior team of individuals by exploiting mistakes, using a few gadgets, getting a 100 percent emotional effort and by playing with precision to an ultimate team pitch.

I once saw a Chicago prep title game played in Soldier Field. One team was unbeaten in 11 games, owned a 210-pound line, had six youngsters headed for major universities and enjoyed a huge advantage in depth. The other team had lost twice, its lines averaged out to 177 pounds and it had only one major college prospect. In the end the smaller team had completely out-maneuvered the huskier outfit and had won going away. In fact, it had almost turned into a route.

The difference: the precision and sharp blocking and the intelligent game plan of the smaller team which neutralized the larger foe with a varietyof men in motion, quick-reacting penetration and by keeping the other team off-balance.

You might ask if our goal to win national recognition, what happens when we lose a game or two early in the year, eliminating hopes of post-season playoff action?

Excellent question. We tell our St. John's teams that lost early and forfeited national acclaim that now our goal is no less modest: win the rest, finish strong, build momentum that can be carried into the first game next year. I point out several choice examples where teams like Alabama, Notre Dame, USC and Penn State have lost early and still won acclaim by getting off the turf and surging on.

The personal satisfaction of seeing your team eliminate mistakes which contributed to early losses is a beautiful thing. Perhaps not the thrill of winning them all, but something which can enhance the spirit and individual pride; something you can look back on and say, "We proved ourselves as the year went on." It's really quite wonderful that the football season is long enough to give a stout team time to vindicate itself. I tell our players that nothing is older than yesterday's headlines—win or lose. The only thing that really counts is today's game—not what happened yesterday.

Today's players, I find, place a great deal of value on turning the tide around. It is profoundly true that sometimes victory tastes sweeter after the sour taste of defeat. I can say honestly that in over 30 years of coaching I never had a team finish a year that didn't look forward to continuing next year, that didn't feel we would be a better squad because of any defeats.

This, of course, is not true of a team that suffers a demoralizing season. When you lose faith in yourself and your coach and team, turning around a team can be extremely difficult. For the coach, the most difficult thing is to make his players believe in themselves and himself. The coach of a losing team in a disastrous season has to examine himself, too. Can his nerves and health stand the strain? What's it doing to his home life? If he finds himself doubting his ability and taking it out on his family, it is time to change course. Only a man who says, "We lost this year but we will storm back next year!" belongs in the coaching profession.

The ultimate optimist can't be a dreamer but he must be a practical fire-eater who believes in his ability. He must, as we said earlier, believe he can sell his system. If he feels that his confidence has been eroded to a point where he can't awaken the spirit that says, "We will win!" and say it with confidence, he is not long for the coaching world.

An old friend who lost 14 of his last 19 games before resigning told me, "I've aged 10 years in two years. I've alienated my family. I've created enemies with a bad personality on campus. The more I lost, the harder I tried, until everything I touched fell apart in my hands."

Nothing is sadder than a battered, losing coach, losing his sense of perspective. It is still a game, although it can be a chilling way to earn a living. But when the time comes that a boy's game is ruining a man's health and imparing his relationships with family and friends, then no goal is worth the impact.

I have felt empty moments. A few years back after a mediocre 5-4 season I pondered the inevitable question: Was I losing it? Had I over-stayed my time? Was the game passing me by? I pondered and reflected for weeks until, Terry Haws, a fine friend, reminded me that if I never won another game in the next decade I would still be above the .500 mark in coaching. This little thought worked wonders. I relaxed. I even laughed at myself.

Goals. Every man has different goals. Every football coach has different goals. I conceded that trying to win national championships every time out may not be all that practical. But I never want to set a lesser goal for my young men. I don't care if we lose 70 percent of the players and our quarterback throws underhanded, I tell them that they have the potential to out-smart, out-think and out-maneuver any team that they play.

Graduation:

"I judge a school's athletic program on only one important count: how many of the players graduate? That's the bottom line."

In an opening game a few years back we played a team which had a game under its belt, which owned a sophisticated passing attack and which was primed to bury us under an avalanche of emotional fury. On the opening reception, the other team marched and threw for 88 yards in 10 plays and we looked mismatched. But our captain, Greg Miller, a burly tackle, came over to me on the sidelines and said, "No worry. We'll have that outfit figured out by the second quarter."

WEDDING DAY IN 1956 also was Valentine's Day for proud John and his lovely bride, Peggy Dougherty.

A BLUSHING BACHELOR, John met nurse Peggy and her mother at a 1955 graduation at nursing school.

Well, we never did figure them out. But our own offense electrified me. After two weeks of drills it went out and ran and threw for 545 yards and 37 points. We won a thriller. I asked the captain if he thought he had figured out the rivals' offense, which had rolled up 490 yards?

"Not really. But we'll know how to handle the next passing team we face."

That's the St. John's way. Learn, keep your chin up, always look ahead.

Goals are the symbols sometimes reached by detours.

What they say about Gag:

"A master of detail and knowledge of the game. That's Gag. I was there in Gag's early years with people like Chuck Froehle, Dean Hall and Harry LaRose. The thing that I remember most is that Gag always seemed about a game ahead of us. He was constantly looking ahead. Many times I heard him bark at the pass defense, 'Who in hell is that guy missing assignments?' We'd try to give him the wrong name. There was always humanity connected with Gag's coaching.

"I doubt if there ever was a coach who made you keep your feet on the ground. He's one in a million. I remember such little things as a fresh end running for a pass that was thrown far over his head. He had his arms outstreched for about 10 yards. Gag blistered him. 'You're creating wind resistance with those arms. Don't put them up until the last second.' Little things make the difference and Gag is tuned to them. He taught me that fortitude will always get you through life when your back is to the wall."

Wayne Hergott

"I remember most Gagliardi's recruiting ability. He has the ability to recruit each athlete as if he were going to be the key player for years to come. Certainly this is reflected in the team he fields with no scholarships. He carries this interest through whether you are on the first team or the fifth team. You always seem to feel special, an intricate part of the team and a close friend of John's.

"Frankly, I don't remember that many games. I do remember the long hours we viewed films. Nobody could watch more people doing more things than John. In the movie room he was a consummate craftsman."

Jack Karnowski

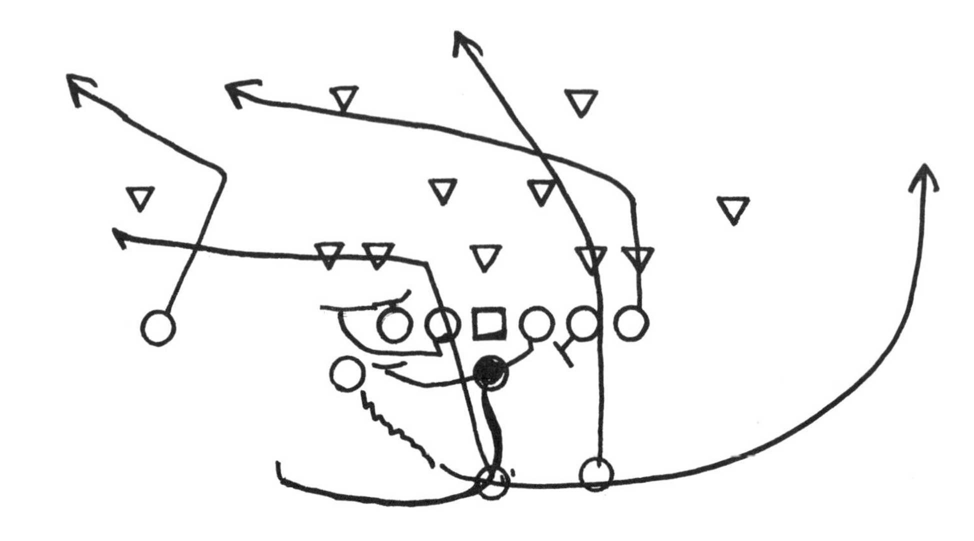

Bootlegger's Delight

Gridiron historians claim they call this pet play of mine a "Bootlegger's Delight" and you can envision the bootlegger sneaking around the corner with the flask on his hip.

This is a beautiful companion play to the fullback trap and the sweep. All of these should originate with the same look. All of them should stop the defensive men in their tracks for a moment, trying to sort out the eventual strike—or keep them bewildered and befuddled, guessing at what it holds in store.

It is called the "bootleg" because the quarterback, after faking to the fullback or slotback, hides the ball on his hip. He can then run or pass, but we have had extraordinary success with this play running.

We have used it on an average of 35 times a year and it has gained, over the decades, an average of nearly eight yards. It has broken up close battles and it has sealed the doom on insurance touchdowns.

I recall one near-perfect execution when Terry Hartman fooled everyone in the arena and went into the end zone untouched in our second NAIA national championship game in Augusta, Georgia. That was the day we defeated Linfield of Oregon 33-0 and this play helped greatly in the destruction. It was our first touchdown of the game and Don Nett, the running back, carried out his fake like the consummate actor.

This play is like the tentacles of an octopus. It can hit you in eight different ways. There are five receivers and the quarterback who can run and if you want to go further you could add another two or three wrinkles.

This is an actor's play. Everyone must perform his role. The faker must have his timing and form down pat. The blockers can't give anything away with their eyes or feet position.

Quarterbacks with any agility love the bootleg. Paul Schmidt and Jeff Norman were two players who preferred to run rather than pass. It really can turn into a quarterback sweep. Notice the two guards leading the blocking. It can become a powerful weapon hitting at the flanks and, because of the run-pass option, the defensive men can't commit that quickly. If they do they take themselves out of the play.

The pulling guards are extremely important. I recall that Ed Donatelle and John Kessler were extremely gifted in clearing the way with good speed and accurate, well-timed blocks.

It was quarterback Dennis Schleper in 1982 leading the nation in passing for us and much of it came off his play. A particular favorite of his was to fake the run and then find our superlative running back, Ricky Bell, coming out of the backfield. Bell weighed nearly 205 pounds and had tremendous hands. He played the entire senior season without giving up the ball on the fumble although he'd catch or run with the pigskin as much as 25 times a game. In one game, Bell caught 12 passes—six of them developing off this bootleg play.

Oh, how I recall the cunning manner in which players like Pat Pederson and Scott Edstrom and Pete Rockers and Jeff Pederson and Ken Roering and Mike Grant gobble in biggies from running back to tight end to break up so many games.

There are, of course, technically right spots for this play. Psychologically, I suppose you would hope it came in the place where the defense might begin to over-react. Perhaps late in a good drive; perhaps when the game is furiously fought and dead-even and the foe might be tempted to gamble on defense.

Of course, the quarterback has to have the instinct. But the beauty is the maze of receivers. I recall split ends like Dave Arnold and Todd Watson and Chuck Williams performing beautifully and with sure-handed poise.

We have always felt on this play during one of our championship years that if quarterback Norman could make the big fake to run and then stop and get the ball to Schmitz coming out of the backfield, that my only worry was the conversion.

I have some interesting figures on the play. Over the last 10 years, the bootleg option has completed passes at a 55.8 percent rate for an average gain of 13.5 yards. Running plays off it produced average gains, as I point out, of over eight yards per carry. In fact, every time we have used this play, it has averaged nearly nine yards.

You might ask, why not use it even more? Because it is a play with a surprise element, and surprises are no longer surprises if they are used too much. But seven or eight times a game, this play has been very rewarding.

Peers needle me that St. John's has used this play since we scrimmaged General Custer's troops on their way out to the Little Big Horn. I know one thing, it is a bread-winner for us. No play gives you more potential game-breakers or touchdown getters.

I'm sure if the bootleggers of old used it in the Roaring Twenties, they gave the cops a merry chase.

3

The Theory Behind Gag's 'Social' Practices

Before an all-star college vs. pro football game in Soldier Field not long ago, Southern California coach John McKay had his practice likened to a country club. His simple explanation: "Why get hurt battering yourself."

I have long championed that theory. Let me explain what happened one day a few years back when a young prospect from a wealthy family first looked at our practice field, sans sleds, blocking dummies and any sign of apparatus outside the goal posts. The young fellow called his father and said urgently, "Geeze, Dad, this place is really hard up. They don't even have any practice equipment. You gotta shell out a few dollars to get them in business!" The father had trouble understanding when I explained, "We work against ourselves. We're our own dummies. We really don't need any equipment. We work out in shorts most of the time."

Let me explain that perhaps my practice philosophies go back to the days that I coached track. I never coached the sprinters as I would the distance men. Football is not a marathon. The players are moving at full speed only three minutes per game; say 60 plays at three seconds each. Think of that! In an hour battle the players are moving at maximum only for three minutes. The plays sometimes last only eight-tenths of a second!

That's the time element. Now let's look at the ground coverage facet. Outside of special teams, the average player is covering only a few yards per play. And on defense, we tell them, make it a lot less than that. But the vital point: the game is made up of quick, disciplined thrusts and bursts of energy and then you reorganize in the huddle. How you walk to the scrimmage or how you line up is nothing. My teams looked almost lackadasical coming out of the huddle; no serpentine snake lines or clapping of hands. This is not the time to put on a show. This is the time to think and build energy for the next burst. We have beaten many teams that looked positively beautiful coming out of huddles. We just try not to get in each other's way.

The huddle is the mental part of the game when you draw a deep breath and clear your head and let the mental capabilities take over. It is a time to charge the battery; to reassess quickly your mistakes or anticipate your next move on the opponent.

Now, please consider this startling figure; in a nine-game season our players must get ready for only 27 minutes of actual physical expenditure. That means that the player does not have to be imbued with the stamina of a cross-country runner or a steeplechase horse or a 15-round boxer. The footballer must have a different kind of condition; one that gets him ready for the three-second thrust...a quick rest...another thrust.

Consequently, I see no reason for gruelling practice routines which risk injury. It has been established that close to 70 percent of all football injuries are directly traceable to the practice field. We can't control injuries, but we certainly can control the degree of risk in practice.

So we agree that it's the disciplined burst of energy repeated over 50 times that controls the result of football games. So our practice drills are not aimed at durability or being able to bench-press 450 pounds. We spend a good deal of time looking at the films. We block people—but not too hard. We spend our time polishing plays. We work on execution and timing. We delight in spending hours just running patterns and enjoying the flow of the game. I'm continually asked what specific drills we use. I don't have specific drills.

One day we might install two new plays for a particular type of defense we expect to see. I transfer the small play cards to a larger blackboard or show the cards to my quarterbacks. We all walk over the new perspective. Then we run it—over and over. We try to build confidence through precision. It wouldn't help us one iota to knock down the would-be tacklers. We don't need to punish ourselves to get ready to punish the rival.

Spurt...burst...explode. We hammer home the fact that for a 240-pound blocker to do his job he doesn't have to carry muscles on muscles and run dazzling sprints. All he has to do is get off the mark, travel two or three yards and make sharp, solid contact for a split second. He begins to believe as he rehearses his role with a minimum of contact. Repetition—not mauling a reserve—is what is all important in the St. John's way.

Our films, like any salesmanship I use, are designed to instill in the team confidence in the St. John's way. I constantly show old Johnnies films of classic victories. A young man may ask, "But that guy was really good? Can I do it?" I tell him the man was not Superman from Krypton. It was just another sophomore or junior who believed he could do it.

I repeat over and over that they can win by doing a few ordinary things extraordinarily well.

Something else that seems to amaze laymen. I have operated through the years with a paucity of assistants. Now I use two or three. I have coached teams with just one. Last year a young rival coach, who happened to have 14 assistants, remarked to a newspaperman, "That Gagliardi must use a wand. I've got all these assistants and he's got a 70-year-old monk and the janitor."

It was a compliment, but I learned something years ago any high school or college coach might use effectively if he truly believes: I let the players teach other players! That's right. I will gather in 18-20 veteran offensive men and run them through two days or so of intense polishing. They will, in turn, pass on their techniques to another

18-20 less experienced men on the third day. They will, in turn, pass on their knowledge to another group the next day. In a week, I can pass our techniques through 100 men.

That might sound incredible on the face of it. But for over 25 years I've had so many players out for the squad there was no way I could teach them individual techniques. So my seniors and veterans have obliged by teaching the new recruits.

It works beautifully. They enjoy being "the boss." They take pride that I trust them enough to show the newcomers the blocking angles and how to get off the mark. I honestly believe that a veteran player can teach a neophyte as well or better than a coach. It becomes a matter of pride.

One of the reasons for the success of this type of teaching is the fact I have stayed pretty much with the same blocking techniques for over 30 years. The same blocks that were bringing us national championships in the 1960s are working for us today. We keep it simple. We keep it clean. We keep insisting that any block can be mastered through disciplined effort and repetition.

Another thing, when we run our early offensive drills, I don't even have the defensive men on the field. I want our offense to build up confidence which tells them they are unstoppable—even if they are running only against themselves, the wind and imaginary foes. Again precision and timing to me are more valuable than butting heads.

A young recruit told me one time, "I'm still running the plays in my dreams and I never get tackled." Great. I would much prefer to send a man into battle who believes every time he carries the ball it will work just like practice, rather than have him limping into a game after having been hammered in scrimmages all week.

The veterans teach the youngsters and nobody gets on the field until he has proven he has learned the St. John's way from an older player. When a starter or veteran tells me, "The new guy is OK," only then does he join the drills on the field. It has always amazed me how quickly one player can teach another. So I reallly don't need a lot of assistants. I have two dozen or more "assistants" among the players implementing my blocking techniques.

The blocking, like I said, is so simple the average player can pick up the fundamentals in 15 or 20 minutes.

It is constant repetition and constant selling. I tell our linemen that we have had offensive backs set NCAA small college records. We then emphasize that no back is better than the linemen opening the holes.

It is fallacy that we have absolutely no contact. We have controlled contact or instant contact—about what you get in touch football. Live people are better than dummies. Dummies have no resiliency or maneuverability. It's like a boxer. He can hammer the heavy bag all day. I compare that to heavy scrimmaging. But the boxer learns nothing about speed or reactions from laboring on the heavy bag. For reflexes he needs a moving target. We block one-on-one, people blocking, but with no heavy equipment and no hammering a man into the ground.

We absolutely NEVER scrimmage. I'm proud that there has never been a legitimate tackle made on the St. John's practice field in over 20 years. Incredible, I suppose, but planned that way. We go 11 men against 11 men, creating constant situations we expect to see during a game. We execute from outside the 40 and inside the 10 and all over the field.

Meanwhile, long ago, we gave away the old St. John's practice pants, sleds and dummies to high schools and reformatories. Our players like to smile that they are capable of playing the roughest game known to man in sweat suits or shorts. Again salesmanship. We tell our young men that they are the only school we know of which practices football without football equipment—another unique attribute which makes the players feel their team is something special.

Now you ask, logically, what of the impact of actual game hitting on a team using only touch-football drills?

Honestly, I am gripped by the cold, chilling hand of anxiety every time the opening whistle blows. Earlier in my career I'd awake in a cold sweat having visions of our players all being carried off the field on the opening kickoff.

In reality, they seem to welcome the collision of bodies. Tim Schmitz, our great fullback, told me, "I feel almost like a caged, angry lion getting loose the day of the game." Another explained, "It's great to let this storehouse of anticipation and energy build for a week. I can hardly wait for the first contact."

I honestly feel it has hurt us a little in the early moments in some games where we might have been too charged up. Other times I have felt we needed a few minutes to adjust. But, on the positive side, we have always been strong fourth-quarter finishers, We have always been stretch runners. I feel that we come to the game without the little sores and ailments that teams seem to carry as the result of tumultuous practice skirmishing.

I have never heard it said a St. John's team didn't like contact.

I think that best serves as credentials for our light drills. Perhaps I should not say "light" drills. For actually we run through our plays perhaps more often than others with a demanding look at the precision and the timing and the reactions.

At every clinic I attend, high school coaches will ask, "Is this method of practicing right for me?"

I firmly believe the system can be applied to high schools with the same success. There is no need for constant head-banging. High school coaches always tell me the same things: they lose games by fumbling high snaps from center, penalties, pass interceptions, dropped balls. It's surely errors and missed assignments which plague prep coaches most. Rarely do I hear a coach say that the foe was bigger than his team or completely out-personneled him.

So it goes back to the premise that you can win football games by execution, the elimination of mistakes—not by out-slugging the opposition.

High school teams could follow our St. John's system; stress situations, repetition of plays, emphasizing that the game of football is predicated on the timing and execution. Of course, high schoolers must spend more time on the basic fundamentals of blocking and tackling because they are still learning, if they have not had pre-prep experience. But again, I believe high school seniors can teach high school frosh quickly the basic arts; then it is up to the coach to inject the intangibles of pride and confidence and belief in the system—and that comes from constant play-drills without heavy contact.

Again. Salesmanship. Selling the belief that "our way wins." Save the hitting for the games, generate confidence and polish—not muscles.

Remember please: I never refer to our practices as "easy." That is the furthest thing from the truth. They are not punishing physically—but they are demanding mentally. I've had players say, "Coach, I heard about your 'easy' practices but I'm dead tired when I am through with two hours of your drills." Exactly. I'm happy to hear that. They aren't limping, but they are tired mentally. They are growing in the mind. They are learning. Learning can be a tiring experience—as much as shoveling coal. But each time your mind absorbs another point, the process becomes easier.

I think it is probably true as someone said that after my practices the players still have fresh bodies but tired minds. Beautiful. The mind feeds the body our messages. Eventually that mind stores up amazing quantities of knowledge and opinions. I want our players to know our system from top to bottom and know that their teammates do, too. Opinion wise, it goes back to every player believing in the St. John's way.

What they say about Gag:

"I guess the thing that strikes me about Gag is that we are better friends after I left school. I had a chance for a tryout with the Washington Redskins and John spent a lot of time making sure I had a good connection with Vince Lombardi. He has heart. A giant heart. I think his basic values surround the trust you put in your teammates and friends.

"John is a great coach on the field, a trusted friend off the field. His coaching goes far beyond the game of football. It embraces the game of life."

Tom Schutta

"Gag is the master at putting football in the proper perspective at St. John's. It's not just the importance of playing well, it's the importance of doing well in the classroom. He has the perfect blend: you get the whole milieu of the school from sports to education to the spiritual. Gag knows the proper blend of what should go into the college athlete, from the tough film sessions to the classroom to the prom."

Bill DeWitt

"Gag and I go back to double dates. As I look at his accomplishments, I believe he is foremost a character builder and value reinforcer. I sent a son to play for him. No greater tribute can a father give a coach because that coach becomes a surrogate father to the boy. My son learned discipline, values, pride, desire and humor. Gag mixes the points beautifully. He can be tough—but he can be tender; honest but compassionate. I can think of nothing a father can do more important than have a son play for The Gag."

Norb Berg

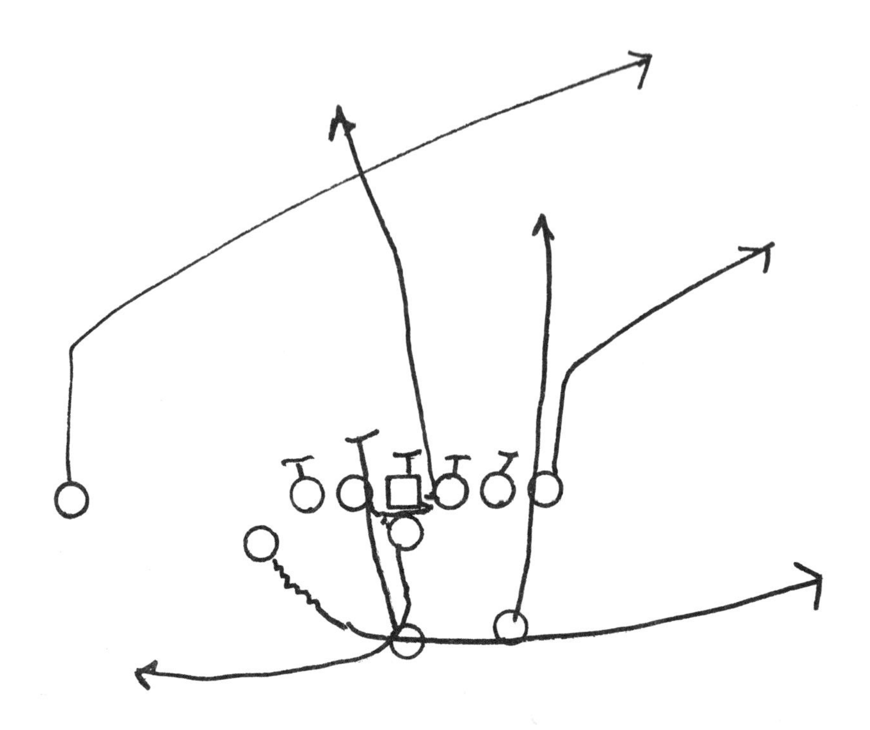

Guards Become Big Play Men

You've probably heard about the guard whose girl friend was coming to watch him practice for the first time. He asked the coach if he might play end for one play and catch a pass. The coach agreed, and so they threw him a pass. He caught it and romped down the sidelines where a defensive back got hold of his pants by the waist and pulled them all the way down around his ankles. Embarrassed beyond belief, the poor guard tried to cover his plight from his girl friend. The coach chuckled and shouted, "That's OK, Bill—It's the first big showing you've made all year!"

I'm sure most guards feel they never get to make a showing. They're usually in the middle of the action but it's always some handsome, sleek running back or big end who gets the raves and the plaudits. The fans know the guards are there, but nobody is really sure what they do.

In this play, everyone remembers the guards. They have the fun. It actually gets the guards into a ball-carrying role. We've used it perhaps a dozen times over the years. It's a wing-dinger and nobody is quite sure what happened when it's over. Hopefully the defense is the most frustrated. When it does work, it's dynamite.

This is actually a guard-around play. The quarterback slips the ball to the pulling left guard and then carries out his fake to the slot-back who pretends to run to his right. Depending on the defense, you can also pull the right guard and make him the hero of the moment.

After the guard gets the ball, he keeps a straight face and hides behind the center. That is, until he thinks the coast is clear. Oh yes, don't forget: to make this play legal, the guard must be behind the line one yard. His shoulders must also be facing the foe's goal-line. This is not difficult if he pulls deep enough. It is an all or nothing at all play: it makes great heroes or it can make the coach a bum. But it's fun and worth the try.

Believe it or not, but we have used it in national championship games. Two great guards at carrying the ball were Dave Honer and Lyle Mathiesen. Both tried it several times in key situations and gained big yardage.

A warning: the guards must wait long enough for the defense to clear and not panic and turn into a horde of tacklers. The fullback fake need not be very good: just enough to protect the open spot where the guard pulled out. That's because we don't want to attract too much attention to the spot where the guard will be hiding. It will either boggle the mind or cause the biggest traffic jam west of Times Square on New Year's Eve.

Sense of humor:

"If you can't laugh at yourself, you are in terrible shape to face the world. Every time I take myself seriously, my wife Peggy will remind me of a couple of gosh-awful defeats or a couple of real lucky breaks. The man who thinks he can control himself and others in every way better learn to laugh a little or he's headed for a serious crack-up."

I thought this one up while manicuring the fender of a blue Pontiac back in my father's garage in Colorado when I was 17 years old. It worked for 20 yards the first time I tried it. Over the years it has been a pleasant surprise and has made yardage perhaps 70 percent of the time. It is a fooler. But the greatest part of it: the guards have a little fun. They get a chance to make that showing without losing their pants.

P.S. They also learn a lot of respect for the ball carriers. And, oh yes, it can create a rhubarb. I had one rival coach running onto the field. He thought the center had carried the ball. Another time a coach reacted so violently, he fell over the bench trying to get to the officials to lodge a protest. I beat a heated rival one time 25 years ago and the coach refused to speak to me at the conference meetings later that season.

But try it. Football is a game. The basics are necessary. The fundamentals are required. But after your team has mastered a dozen or so rudimentary plays, add a little razzle-dazzle. At least it sure makes practice that much more fun.

And, oh yes, his mother can finally recognize that guard.

4
Football Means Solving Problems

Let's get this straight: I can't win with 97-pound weaklings. You have to be big ENOUGH. I can't ask a 170-pound lineman to continually take on a 230-pound foe for 30 minutes. I simply say, be big enough. At some point in every game you must match the rival physically. But we never lose because we are not big enough; we lose because we are not good enough. We lose when we make more vital mistakes than the opposition.

It is not the great plays you make which win games; it is the mistakes you DON'T make that wins games. Football, perhaps even more than hockey or basketball, is a game of mistakes. The perfect game has never been played.

There are perhaps an average of three to one more mistakes made in a game than great plays. Consequently my coaching philosophy has always been: don't worry about making the great play. Worry more about minimizing the mistakes.

Solving problems. The coach who approaches a daily practice and doesn't believe he has a problem is only fooling himself. He's living in a dream world. Alonzo Stagg once told some young coaches that he never felt he had ever prepared a team perfectly for any game. There was always an element of work left undone. You only hope the other team has entered the fray with more loose strings.

A young coach once told me before a game, "John, I've done everything I can. I have to believe we're as ready as we can be mentally and physically." No coaching master has ever lived who can anticipate and obliterate all the possible weaknesses of his team in four or five days of practice. You try to eliminate as many urgent problems as you can. You only hope your level of intensity and emotion and thoroughness is better than the rival. Never enter a game expecting to win without mistakes. Only hope you limit your mistakes and force the opposition to make more. Mistakes are what decide winners. Imagine a tennis game without a service break. It would go to eternity.

Capitalize and exploit...capitalize and exploit...Force errors and exploit more than the opposition. I have no figures, but I believe we have won as many games by forcing a mistake in the final period than we have by building our own momentum in a long march.

Only this year I noticed a quote from a high school coach who said he could not ask for a better group of physical specimens. But in three weeks he had been decimated by injuries. His program collapsed. He went in believing that he had all the manpower he needed. He had based his program on physical advantages.

Let's look at the problem of weight discrepancies—which many high schools with small enrollment face. I have told such teams that 22 Adonises with 22-inch necks still can't win if those massive muscles are missing assignments. So to solve the weight disadvantage, minimize the importance of power and, as I said earlier, point out that smartness isn't sold in 220-pound packages.

This idea of weight programs is wonderful for the psyche—but I also examine our national champions, most of whom never had weight programs. I constantly examine how my athletes are affected by weight programs. Some become more confident and seem to have sold themselves on the theory that it has improved their stamina. But I find the 200-pounder who is thinking clearly, getting off the mark making sharp and clean contact, can dislodge the strongest weight-man who ever lived. It is still timing, precision and combativeness based on intelligent operations.

I had a 175-pounder who, through weight programs, blossomed into a 220-pounder, but he lost a shade of that quickness which was so vital. He went from an exciting breakaway back to a rather average linebacker. Weight programs are sophisticated and endearing to many and certainly a help to the 200-pounder who must weigh 230 to attract college and pro scouts' attention. They serve a great purpose for a lot of youngsters. But they didn't win football games any more than they guarantee homerun hitters.

Size:

"Of course, today you must have big players. But never discount the 170-pounder with fire in his eye. They have contributed as much to my record as the muscle-men. It's nice to have a 22-inch neck. But I'd prefer a bulging 22-inch brain."

Feisty Billy Martin has always said that hitters have hostility on their minds and lightning in their reactions. Size helps, but it didn't help Gil Hodges in the World Series when he became the goat because he couldn't find the pellet.

So weight is a problem that sometimes is more on the mind of the coach than an actuality in the conception of the game plan. He must convince his players that they will win with precision and timing...reactions and resources; that they have more of these qualities than any amount of size can handle. So much for a problem that seems to disturb many young coaches whose squads lack beef.

Fumbling is a problem that is so devious and so difficult to diagnose that the best solution seems to be not to think about it. Let me give you an example: spirited young coach Joe Salem of the University of Minnesota came to his position from Northern Arizona where his teams had one of the finest records for not fumbling in the country. Yet in his first year his Gophers had repeated fumbles which hurt. Joe said, "I can't explain it. We're doing the same things we did at Northern Arizona but here our gifted people are dropping the ball."

Fumbleitis is an ellusive, deadly foe, full of caprice and injustices.

Oklahoma's Barry Switzer wins and accepts the fact that his amazing option game will fumble—but that it will neutralize the affect with consistent long gains. I've had teams that fumbled and teams that didn't. I would tell the fumbling teams that it is a matter of percentages. After one game in which we lost the ball four times I said quietly, "We've had our fumbles for the season. No more." We didn't lose a fumble for the next five games. Another time I told a macaroni-fingered runner to remember that if he dropped the ring, when he got married, to kick it forward. He became a human wrench.

It can be a mental thing. Of course we teach the runners to cover the points, tuck in under the arm, shift the ball with control and always think about protecting the football no matter how violent the collision. I had a young back rocked nearly senseless one time. He and I inquired how he was feeling. He looked up and smiled, "Great, coach. Notice I didn't lose the ball."

Let's say that the problem is lack of passing. I had a quarterback who would have had trouble passing the salt. But he could ball handle. We built our attck around sleight-of-hand handoffs. He became a magician. I told him,"You will never be a passing star but you can lead. If you only complete three or four a game, you can still direct our team with that ball handling." He didn't get many headlines, but we tried to solve a potential problem by instilling in this man the belief he could be the best ball handler in the country. I had trouble following his feints. He was like a master boxer—using his head and shoulders and hips. Again, a case of selling. His morale was low early on because of his erratic passing. Later he bloomed with wonderful self-assurance as he led us with deception and cunning.

Actually, I have fun with problems. This may sound strange. But let's say we are meeting a finely-tuned passing team. I will gather my defense round me and ask, "How do you think we should handle all this passing?" The players or my assistants may volunteer a few suggestions. Then I might tell them what I have felt for years.

"Let's say Joe Namath was out here throwing to our receiver with no coverage. He might hit eight out of 10, but one would be a little high or wide or too fast and one would be dropped, at least. That means 20 percent of the time Joe Namath would self destruct. Let's say now it's a game situation. If we get a little rush on Joe, he's got to throw one out of 10 away or too low or have it deflected, right?

"Now let's say he trips getting up or slips a little or can't quite get the right grip on one out of 10 plays. Now he's down to 60 percent, right? Now let's say we're reading the patterns pretty well and we are in position to knock down or bat way or foul up the receiver on just two out of the 10 plays. Namath is down to 40 percent, right? And he can't beat us with just 40 percent, right?"

It's as simple as that. No matter how slow, inexperienced or ill-conceived a defense, the passing team must make one great play out of 10 passes to reach 50 percent. Anything less and they rarely will beat you. I have our players solving the pass defense problem by figuring that the greatest passer in the business will misfire 40 percent of the time at least. The other 20 percent of the time we have to do some things soundly and with confidence to turn the percentage in our favor.

This philosophy takes the strain off a defense, which might figure it is deadly responsible for every passing completion. I try to sell our defense that the best passing in the country cannot keep marching against us forever. An interception, I point out, is a beautiful bonus and brings us maybe 50-60 yards in control yardage. Territorially, two interceptions should turn most games around. Three interceptions generally can secure a victory if you are moving the ball.

So I urge other coaches not to put a premium on the strength of the rival. Air games have a tendency to throw young teams into panic. They must be sold on the idea that fine passing teams have a number of things that can blow up in their faces. Tennessee's Bob Nyland used to say, "Three things can happen when you put the ball in the air—and two of them aren't good."

This is not to detract from the air arm. We use it, too. Half of our teams have been built around passing; half around running. But, when we did throw the ball, I emphasized that we can let a good team turn it against us; that we must use it scrupulously and maintain the surprise move for the long strike rather than attempt pure ball control via the air.

Teams that expect to have trouble in the air, find trouble there. Teams that expect to turn the rival air game into a boomerang, win.

Problems abound. And every game presents new ones. But a problem is a challenge. No coach should enter the profession if he doesn't constantly accept challenges. Lack of experience. Nothing new. It hits every team every three or four years. I tell an inexperienced team, "You are not entering a season of learning; you are entering a new era in St. John's winning. We don't expect to make this a learning experience or just build character. We will continue to win."

On the matter of injuries, I tell the man replacing the wounded player; "You are good enough to start. You would not be on the St. John's squad if you were not. Here is your chance. I'm sorry about the injury but if you play the way I think you can, the injured man may have trouble getting his job back when he returns."

I use a laughable slogan in my coaching, "Don't go to the outhouse because your job will be gone when you return." It simply emphasizes the belief that every man on the squad has some kind of God-given talents. Implement these with desire. Show him your confidence. Let him see your trust. Pat him on the rear and turn him lose with the words, "I believe in you or you wouldn't be in the lineup." Rarely will a player fail to respond.

The problems of personality clashes. Sure, we've all experienced them. But I lay down a tough code before every season: "You are all St. John's men. No one can win without the other. We are a team built on synchronization and timing. Any part that throws us off will not be tolerated."

Every team has loud-mouths; every team has braggarts...most teams harbor jealousy. It must be snuffed out at the beginning.

I have said that the great player thinks first about the team. I remember a baseballer who used to sulk when his team won if he didn't go four-for-five. Sure baseball is more individualistic, but I was happy to hear young World Series record-hitter Paul Molitor of Milwaukee tell me one night, "I still have to think about the team first to be comfortable with myself. The man who thinks constantly about his own figures burns himself out. Be a team man and the figures take care of themselves."

Molitor knew whereof he spoke. He opened five seasons for the Brewers in five different positions. Rather than destroy his individuality, he just signed a five-year $4.5 million contract. Team performance pays off for Molitor.

I tell the few young men we get who insist on setting their sights for pro football, "The scouts will find you. Winning teams are never overlooked. Win first, worry about discovery later."

Problems. I told a kicker who was having trouble to think about his girl friend the next time he tried a 30-yard field goal. He said he didn't have one. I said think about fishing. He said he hated it. I said pretend you are showing off at the Fair. Anything, but don't get up tight. Then I whispered, "You know, if this team is doing its job, you should never have to try a field goal. What you get is a bonus after we've scored. No big deal." It hit the trigger button on his psyche. "I've never thought of it that way." He relaxed and became an integral part of the St. John's way.

Now this sounds strange, but I hope the sun never comes up on the day I don't face a football problem. It's like playing the violin. You are always learning. I have never experienced the game in which my team or the foe has not surprised me. I have never faced the day when I said we are perfectly prepared. I hope I never will. For then the mystique will have been lost. Football is a game where you often create your own problems.

I've had teams that score impressively in the first period, were woeful in the second, awesome in the third and clutching in the fourth. Nobody designed that. Nobody implemented that. I've had teams that never got off the ground until the fourth quarter. I certainly never planned that.

Problems are forces that wear like T-shirts. I would feel naked without them.

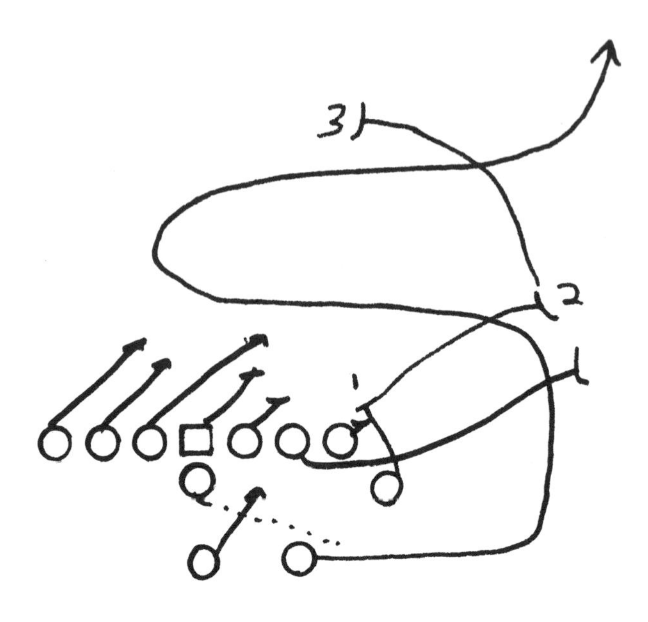

Right Sweep to Eternity

This play is a legend among St. John's foes. I think they'll mostly speak of it in awe. One year in key third-down situations we averaged 12.8 yards with it. It is the backbreaker, Southern Cal has its "student body right" and Oklahoma and Texas have their famed dive series and Stanford has its incredible passing game when it isn't lateraling through bands in the last seconds. But St. John's has the right sweep to eternity.

Over the years this play has won more games for us than any other. We've used it as much as 12-15 times a game. We've used it on good fields and bad; against big foes and small men. Nothing much has changed with it over the years. Styles come and styles go, but when the St. John's team lines up, watch for this one. It exemplifies, perhaps more than any other play, the basic idea behind St. John's football: be sure you always have a weapon and dry ammunition.

It is unique that a tackle pulls and blocks. The fake is made to the fullback and then the quarterback pitches out to the running back who moves out around the right flank.

That pulling tackle is a vital man. And what a thing of beauty to see bruising 210-220-pounders over the years, like Fred Cremer and Mike Collins and John McDowell and Rodger Ludwig and Jim Sexton, leading the back up the field. Some backs would tuck in behind the big blocker. Others would use the blocker as a convoy only until he saw daylight and then veer and slash and streak to other directions of the field.

One particular play is written in indelible ink on the grid history of St. John's. This is the way it happened: Jack Karnowski lined up at wing back and he cracked back on the rival end. That was his first block on a play that sprang Jim Lehman loose on a brilliant run. Lehman got around the corner and cut back, while Karnowski was hustling down to nail the defensive halfback with his second block. Finally, Lehman made one more desperate cut back to the right as he began to break into open territory. Naturally, Jack was pursuing and drilled the last pursuer.

It was one of the few plays in history where a man made three blocks on one play. The quick-thinking Karnowski is still making big plays in the business world and currently is treasurer at the mammoth Control Data Corporation. He's told me, "After that, my ambition was to make four blocks on one play—but the opportunity never arose."

It might be added that Lehman made many dazzling runs for us in the early 1950s. He had a knack of setting up blocks. He also could stop on a dime and give you the change.

The run for eternity is a classic. In the St. Cloud game where Karnowski made his triple sweep, the rival coach joked about it later. "We made Karnowski a man of history—a living legend on one play."

Pulling the tackle adds a dimension. The pure, quick strike of the play is what make it a St. John's trademark. If he wanted to be known for one play, it would be this one. Nothing elaborate. But it's a thinking man's play. The blockers must hit with cleanness and crispness. The runner must decide if he's going to go with the flow or against it. The blockers, like Karnowski, must be alerted to the premise the runner will cut back. The runner must be setting up the final blocks, hopeful of exploding into the open.

It is a play that has won perhaps 40 percent of our games by either exploiting a developing defensive weakness or setting up something else—like the option pass play. Just as the old Minnesota Gophers of Bernie Bierman built around the famed buck-lateral series, it is the right sweep to eternity that holds our attack together.

In one game in the late 1940s, I called it 18 times. It gained yardage 16 times and wound up gaining 188 yards. I decided that day that anything that could work so effectively so often has to be the core of my offense.

5
Eyeballing the Prospects

What kind of players do I look for? I have always tried to live by the credo, "Send me a good boy and I'll try to return you a good man." This puts a tremendous burden of proof on the coach. He still must have material with some raw talent.

First impressions can be so deceiving, yet we are all forced to make judgements on initial contacts. I have had great success over the years with the strong, silent types. But then I've always been a great John Wayne fan. I tend to shy away from the glib talkers. On the field I want a boy whose attention I can command. He might not be a great player, but I am satisfied with the youngster who is a great listener.

I have cultivated this philosophy over the years—that a good listener is usually possessed of good concentration. Oh, how important that ability to concentrate! From safecrackers to athletes to political leaders, nothing is more important than the ability to concentrate.

I have known coaches who claim heart is all important. Well, I would rate that quality right behind concentration. Can you measure heart? No, but there are some strong indicators. I want the boy who doesn't alibi. In fact, the young men with whom I've had the greatest success are totally responsible for their own actions.

When I look at a scouting report, my eyes gravitate first to his scholastic ability. I find a direct correlation between his work in the classroom and his ability to concentrate, accept responsibility and play with heart.

Recently I was interviewing two youngsters within hours of each other. One explained his mediocre senior year by saying, "Most of our squad graduated and I really didn't have much help up front." The other said, "I leveled off my last year but I hope to perform up to my capabilities in college." Just a few words of explanation but they told a mountain of basic differences. The coach must be a good listener, too.

Another day it was two youngsters who were talking about classroom responsibilities and one said, "My record isn't too good...I guess I spent too much time playing sports." Another said, "I'm just beginning to realize how important schoolwork is—and I plan to really work to improve in college." The second youngster has a chance to excel in both the classroom and on the gridiron.

I don't mean a player has to be an A student. But he must show enough initiative to want to improve, to want to learn. A player who can't concentrate in class can't concentrate enough on the field to play the St. John's way. Give me a mediocre athlete with responsibility and desire to learn and the willingness to improve in the classroom, and I'll show you a man who can become a valuable asset to any team.

I look for players who can listen, hold up their end of the study program, seek to improve themselves and have heart. I find that there is a direct parallel between the young men who listen and work well in the classroom with those who show tremendous heart and desire on the field.

That's why I am so proud of our football players' achievements over the years. We have an inordinately large number become leaders in professional fields from doctors to lawyers to businessmen and politicians. We have turned out leaders in finance and communications. I was honored a few years back when the *Chicago Tribune* headlined a series of articles about our football and scholastic program. I told reporters the two ran hand in hand.

I suppose a certain type of young man gravitates toward the serenity and rural atmosphere of St. John's. The Benedictine monks run a tranquil and thoughtful environment, nurturing a good study atmosphere. It is not devoid of social ramifications with the nearby colleges of St. Benedict and St. Cloud, but I have found the young man who wants to play for St. John's is one who appreciates a clear head and the time to ponder solutions to the world's questions.

It is hard to stereotype any player. I have had witty ones who were grimly efficient under pressure. I have coached loners whose rapport grew in wide dimensions as they became a member of a team. I have seen sour personalities become ingratiating under the influence of team cameraderie.

I don't say football can change a young man's personality traits or infuse a weak character with Spartan dedication. But football, like no other game, puts a premium on sharing common goals and body contact and sharing responsibility. There is nothing like it.

When I send out perhaps 100 invitations to young high school prospects in the area, I look at their class percentile. Because of solid admission regulations, a young man should stand in the top 40 percent of his class. Even then he may experience problems. He must be able to afford the tuition, which is considerably more than state institutions! We have work programs and financial aid programs, and we will help the willing student, but his family must be prepared to handle a share of the costs.

Mind:

"Knowing what's inside a player's mind is far more important than his knowing what is on the blackboard."

That means we are limited in the prospects we can attract. I tell them we have two things to offer if they play football: a chance to be with a consistent winner—and a first class education.

If a boy is looking for more, he has not a place in the St. John's system.

You may ask why do I carry so many players—numbering over 100. Simple. I want them all to be a part of the St. John's feeling. I want them all to be proud of their red uniform. I want them to be able to say "I play football for St. John's." Some may never play more than a few minutes. Fortunately, because of our records, we have been able to use most of them at least sparingly.

I would much prefer to spend money and suit up 100 than pour the same monies into tackling and blocking machines. In the end, wearing the St. John's uniform will mean more than running into padded posts.

Study the prospect's eyes. Study his speech when he talks about his parents. There are so many give-aways. I had a boy who said he was coming to school just because "my old man" wanted him to. I discouraged him. Another said, "You've got such a good rep, Mr. Gagliardi, I figure I can get to a bowl with you." Nice to hear, eh. I didn't really want that young man. I told him, "If you come to St. John's, I certainly hope it's more valid than just because I run the football program. Lord, I could be hit by a bus in your second semester."

You can be wrong in early judgements. None of us is Solomon. I interviewed a boy who said, "I don't really think football is for me. Do you mind if I just kind of come out informally? It would be nice to pick up a letter jacket.

Imagine. Here I was talking to a young man who didn't care if he played or not but thought it would be nice to wear a letter jacket. I was amazed two years later when he became a brilliant lineman, playing every game as if it were his last. I asked him how such a monumental change came over him; how he grew to apparently love a sport which he hadn't cared about.

"I guess it's the flavor of the team. It's become a challenge. I feel now that other people need me. I feel responsibility. It's become one of the biggest things in my life."

I guess no more eloquent testimony to the infectious fires of football can be hung on a locker room wall.

Good players come in all sizes, all shapes and in bewildering temperaments. But generally speaking, men who will listen, study and enjoy their friends and teammates—and share, oh, how important that is, share—they are the ones I hope I am lucky enough to find.

An old chaplain once told me he was certain there were no bad football players—just indifferent ones. I am inclined to agree.

I can't condone a coach who crawls for a player. I promise him nothing but the opportunity to try and make a good team, get a good education and make lifelong friends. I offer him only values—not sports cars. I recall what Olympic hockey coaching hero Herb Brooks said one time: "If I have to plead with a boy and make him promises to get him to play on my team, then I don't want him. I want only those who see it as a great opportunity and want to be part of a winning tradition." A man after my own heart.

I get a personal satisfaction and genuine inner thrill from seeing an average player suddenly realize his full potential. This is much more rewarding than just putting the harness on the superior athlete. I love to see young men who think they have limited capabilities, suddenly expand and use gifts they never knew they possessed—and rise to the stars.

The few players who have quit our team over the years or given up in the

DUFFY DAUGHERTY, the great Michigan State coach, is one of Gagliardi's admirers, too.

classroom have hurt me deeply. I hate to lose any of them. Some may only see action in drills or for a few minutes, but I honestly believe the ones who see their careers through, no matter how sparingly they play, are stamped with a dedication ethic that will last forever.

Find the boy who wants to play—and he will play.

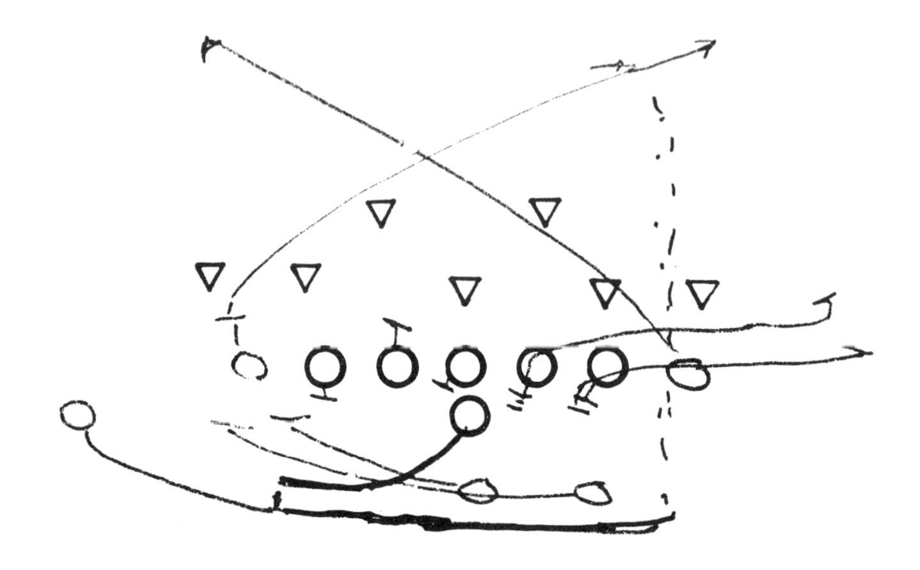

Trickery May Get You Everything

This is the play that always makes the wide receivers smile and the lady fans from the College of St. Benedict's keep coming back to the game. I tell the players the gal fans love this one. It's the kind that brings giggles to children and leaves the old-timers shaking their heads. It's a joy riding to break up any monotony that develops. How does it work in a game? You'd be surprised. At St. John's we've piled over 800 yards with it over the years.

This is a play that seems to work when we need it. We use it an average of just three times a year. But as you can see, the gains over the decades have been substantial. We joke about this one. I tell the wide receivers to forget their hands on this play. Just make sure they've brushed their teeth. Usually they're smiling on its completion and we want bright smiles on our receiving stars.

It's basically a quarterback fake to backs heading left and then the wide receiver comes back against the grain for a reverse. He can then run to his right, or as so many have then preferred, throw a deep pass to the left end cutting across 20 yards downfield.

It's a beautiful play to watch. Bernie Beckman threw many times on this play to Ken Roering and nobody can forget big John Hanowski showing he could throw as well as receive by making Mike Grant his target. This option has almost a hypnotic effect on rivals. They seem to freeze in their tracks.

It is a play that might get you back in the game when everything else seems to be falling apart. It is a play that could be the knockout punch, the real killer in a close game. It is a play where you have to have complete confidence in your wide receiver to throw the ball—at the right man.

Once, after an interception, the wide receiver told me, "John, I've got the hands—but not for passing."

But try this in drills every now and then. It puts life in a team. Oh, sometimes the ball will hang or wobble like a wounded duck. But you'll be surprised how often the receiver has just waited for the chance to throw the football.

In our history, it has produced, I'd say, a dozen touchdowns. I remember one in particular. We worked it for a score in our first national championship game. We also scored on it again in our third national championship battle.

Checking the records, I find that although we have used it only about 90-100 times since I've been here, it has scored 16 touchdowns. That is a high percentage for a play in which the receiver usually throws the ball. It can be a heart-stopper for the fans and a brain-rattler for the defense.

6
Foreign Fields, Weather, Fans and Pep Talks

Like other coaches, I have preferences for how, when and where I would prefer to perform. But the secret is to never let your squad know that it means the slightest iota to the conditions or surroundings.

If we anticipated a bad weather field, I tell the squad we have a tradition of winning in the mud and sleet or snow or hail. If it's cold and horrendously windy, I inform them it was on just such a day we turned Mother Nature into an ally to defeat Prairie View in national action. If it's unseasonably hot, I tell them we have our best performances on opening games in steamy weather; that we always outfinish the opposition.

If it's a night game, I may remind the squad of the time we beat Duluth 60-6 under the lights although we have never practiced under lights.

And, if it's the other team's homecoming game, I recollect vividly the day we defeated an excellent Concordia team 31-0 before their old alumni and they didn't make a first down until the fourth quarter.

Of course, rival crowds can intimidate teams from South Bend to Norman to Baton Rouge. But I tell our forces, the greatest thrill in a game is to take the roars out of the rival crowds, silence it with a surging start. Try to take control early.

Always a new challenge. The time we faced an opening foe which already had played two games, we didn't worry about their experience. I told our forces that we were fresh while they were nursing bruises and sores and would gradually be worn down as the game progressed.

They had us right where we wanted them.

You have to realize in coaching that there is no provision for asterisks after the score saying "Team hot" or "Team cold" or "Loud enemy crowd." You can't explain a loss in the record book with, "No wind at our backs in fourth quarter."

I continually remind our young men that both teams play in the same circumstances. Nobody's tilting the field against us or pouring mud in our shoes. It all goes back to discipline and execution.

Let's get back to night games. The reason that we don't work out under lights is simple: I don't want our team to ever think that the bulbs are going to make a difference. If they don't think about it before the game, they won't think about it during a game. We never give the rivals the solace of thinking the lights will aid their game.

All of these are important little nuances that can affect a team. You must strive to lighten the importance of any believable or feigned advantage the rival uses. Our road record is 71 percent victories. It has never been a major factor. To be undefeated you must win on the road, tame hostile crowds, sometimes escape erratic officiating and play with impervious calm in all kinds of weather. When I hear a young man complain about cold hands, I ask him with a half smile, "Ever see George Gipp in a picture wearing gloves?"

Two years ago we lost just two games—both at home. Drive a stake into my heart and I could not be more aware of the fact you can die in friendly surroundings. I think home fields are the most overrated advantages in the game. Wait for the home field to reward you with a victory and you're destined for defeat.

I recall a game played late in the year when the rival's home field was supposed to stymie our ground game. Well, it did. We got only 167 yards along the ground—far below our average. But here is the punch line: we made 140 of it inside the rival's 40-yard lines—recovering four of their fumbles in the slop which we converted into scores.

Against the great Emporia, Kansas, team in the un-Godly chills at the Twin Cities wind-swept and frozen tundra of Metropolitan Stadium, I reminded the team of the great tradition of the Minnesota Vikings team on the same field and same conditions. I told them, too, that it all worked in our favor. Emporia had the speed but it would be neutralized on the frozen and treacherous turf. We went into the game believing the wind and cold was a comrade in arms and won 54-0.

Another game late in the years with major stakes at hand was played in driving sleet. The ball became as difficult to handle as if it has been soaked in a vat of vaseline. I told our players, "Keep an eye on loose pigskins. Everyone is a potential gamewinner." I think we recovered five fumbles, lost three and scooped up a blocked punt to turn the tide.

I'll never forget how an imposing Southern California team was trapped in a Minnesota blizzard. Its wheels became immobile. Its super sun-stars never blossomed. It eventually became frustrated and bewildered and the Gophers sprung a major upset. But I have to believe the Trojans were beaten at the first sign of snowflakes. Bud Grant, the coach of the Vikings, whom I deeply admire, has said often that the weather and the thought of the weather won more games for him than any stars. Psychologically the field, weather or fans build only as many monkeys as you permit.

For instance, I have been aided in winning games when loud fans actually impaired the signals of their own team. I have seen passing teams pray for sun and a windless day and then detonate in their own game plans. I have seen small teams dominate large teams in the mud, and large teams lose all sense of balance on frozen surfaces.

Which brings up the pre-game pep talks, the dependence on emotions. In a nine-game schedule you can't get by on emotions more than twice in a season.

Actually, I rarely use a "pep" talk before the game. I generally vocalize after the last practice on Friday. I remind the players once more about our basic game plans. Then I ask them to concentrate real hard and try to conjure up all our plays working to perfection; I ask them if they can picture Monday's game films—a sneak preview so to speak. Always picturing the plays working to precision and perfection. I ask them to see themselves winning. I then remind them to keep cool, clear heads and function to the limit of their abilities. I ask them to explode off the line of scrimmage, but always in control.

Then I remind them that all teams point toward us, that this is the major game for most of them. I tell them every game thus becomes that much larger when you wear a St. John's uniform. I remind them that we have usually beaten the up-coming team by out-lasting them, playing with poise and concentrating on making each play in timing drills work as well in the game.

The day of the game, with time running out, we may go over a few vital points. I always remind them that it will take the opposition three things to beat us:

1. They will have to play the greatest game of their lives.
2. They will have to get some monumental breaks and a friendly decision from officials. Even that won't be enough.
3. We have to make some horrible mistakes, like having punts blocked or fumbling deep in our territory.

If we don't make the big mistakes, even a phenomenal game by our foe or controversial calls can beat us.

Here I am trying to completely minimize the potential for the other team to beat us, providing we don't beat ourselves. In other words, I am trying to get across that if we play our normal, tough, dedicated St. John's game, there is virtually no way the other side can win.

In one game I told a team, "The other team is making much of its superior size and home field and the bad weather. Actually, we have the precision and advantage of mobility and weapons, and everything they think they have is playing right into our hands."

Never raise the spectre of defeat. Build confidence—but not overconfidence.

Let me give you an illustration. Let's go back to the national championship game with Towson State of Maryland. The game was played in Alabama. We jumped to a 28-0 lead, but in the fourth quarter they made a fantastic rally to tie the score. With a minute to play, momentum had suddenly turned in their favor. It would have been the spot for a team of weaker character to fold. We were going against a rising tidal wave. But many times I had told this team that St. John's thrives on tense struggles won in the last few seconds.

Calmly and quietly, quarterback Jeff Norman told our team, "We've got all the time in the world. Just like practice." We moved the ball 55 yards in three plays after a fine kickoff return. From this spot we kicked a field goal to win. Included in this counterattack was a wonderful stroke of psychology when Norman completed a pass right in front of their bench—while they were still celebrating tying the score.

Just a few days earlier I was telling some of the squad, "St. John's has been in big games before—enough to know we can win at any time, from any place on the field, against any team." I am sure the squad was thinking along those lines when it actually seemed to welcome the chance to march in the last minute.

I love to tell the teams about the time Augsburg was on the verge of a rousing upset victory over us in Minneapolis. The Augs were ahead 15-14 and had the ball on our two yard line with two minutes to play. Somehow, we grabbed a bobbled ball, the defending hero, Rick Lovett, lateraled it off and Bob Berton, the recipient, lateraled again as we raced to a winning touchdown.

Keep insisting to your team that no matter the score or the grimness of the situation, the impossible is being performed every Saturday on fields all over the country. At St. John's we say the impossible has come to be expected. Again, salesmanship; the idea of turning the other man's advantage or strength actually to a favoring commodity for yourself.

One day I went back over our record and discovered that we had won nearly 10 percent of our games by coming back late in the battle against heavy odds and under abominable conditions. I keep reminding our teams that we may not have the facility of blowing out most teams, but we have ingenious ways and coolness under duress to "steal" many victories which perhaps belong on the other side of the ledger. Fortunately we have been able to develop a core of people on our teams every year which feel we will always find a way.

I cannot emphasize this point too much. I have seen strong teams crumble under a little diversity. I have seen entire offensive and defensive units panic when they fell behind late in the game. The coach is the beacon—the light in the stormy sea. He must show confidence and exude poise regardless of the straits. He must keep up his front to the final whistle.

I have always contended that when a team is down in a hole with time running out and the blue chips piled a mile high against them, then that is when the true worth of a coach is shown. It is not difficult to direct a winning operation. It can be the sign of brilliance to hold a struggling team together, to keep its spirit alive and to instill hope to the final whistle. Those are qualities which exuded from the great generals from Alexander to Patton; a mental toughness and an unquenching optimism. They are the qualities which separate merely good coaches from great coaches.

Most Kentucky Derbies are won in the stretch. Remind your teams of that. When have you seen a National Basketball Association playoff game that was won much before the last three or four minutes? Football comes down, too, to basic mental toughness, the will to believe and survive in the stretch. Nearly one out of five games that I have charted are not decided until the last five minutes.

Now I remind our teams that all Kentucky horses are splendid, valuable thoroughbreds—but only one has the will and heart to win in the gruelling stretch. Stamina, class, confidence breeds winners.

I firmly believe that an indelible mark can be made on your teams to perform even better than they know how on foreign fields, against treacherous weather, aroused teams and loud fans. Welcome the chance to turn adversity into advantage. Like I have said, football is made up of problems. I genuinely love the challenge when the other side THINKS it has the edge.

I love to think of our Johnnies as thoroughbreds. The analogy fits them, I say; they may not have the initial power and speed but if they position themselves right, keep on the game plan, play with patience and controlled inner fury and then make their move at the right time, the finish wire will be theirs. I tell them, that like Derby winners, they are built to handle pressure.

I once saw handicap star John Henry win a $600,000 race at Arlington. I had to smile. He was not a handsome horse. His coloring, stature and demeanor were average. He didn't stand out from the crowd. All he did was win. I don't care how St. John's looks or how it comes out of the huddle or what style it uses or what the critics say about its chances. I just want it to be a thoroughbred winner in all kinds of territory—hostile or friendly.

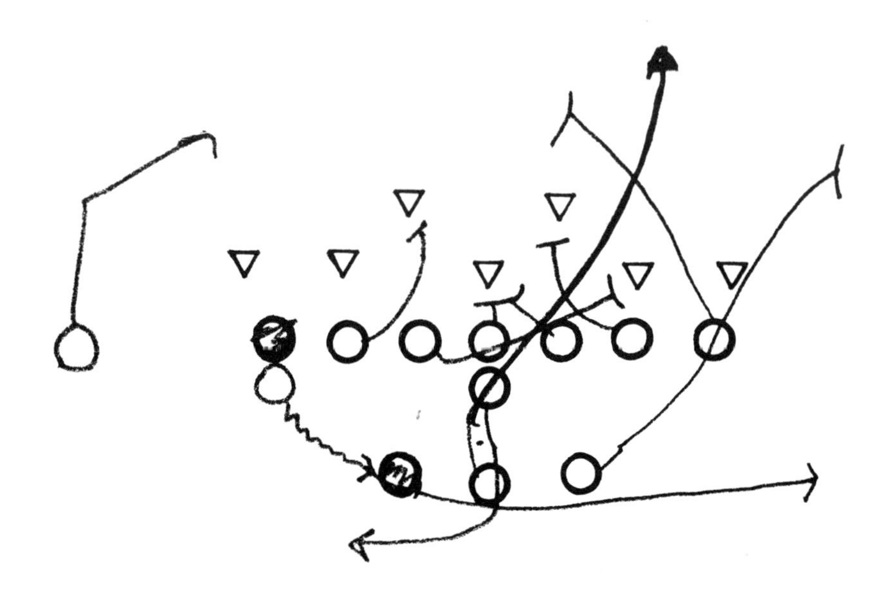

How to Spring the 'Trap'

Guards are people who usually go unnoticed until they are off-side or recover a fumble. Believe me, they are the backbone of a winning team. That's why I love the trap plays. Without the guard's perfect execution, the backs can be buried under an avalanche. This play, of course, is designed when the defense is looking for a pass and the rush is on.

I recall how well Stan Suchta and Rich Froehle used this play to pile up yardage. on our first national champion team. We still use it regularly. Joe Cronin blasted up the middle with this play for large gains and so did Ricky Bell and Tim Schmitz. In one game against a traditional foe, this play was used eight times for over 80 yards. It got two touchdowns as well.

It's a crush to teams' defenses, particularly if they have just come up with a big play. Say they have dumped your quarterback for a five-yard loss and are anxious to destroy the line and pile up another big loss. This is the perfect time for the trap—which is exactly what it is called. The on-rushing linemen are left across the line of scrimmage and then caught in the crossfire of the guards dropping back. Over the years, guards like Ed Donatelle, Dave Honer, Bill Smock and John Kessler were some of our best trappers.

One player told me after he had waylaid a big opposing lineman with the trap three or four times, "That play used regularly could put me in the Hall of Fame." I told him, "Only if the defensive lineman were a lot dumber than I thought."

This is a play that has to be called at just the right time pyschologically. It is a mind-whipper. It sets up other plays. It dresses the table. Use it when the pass and sweeps have been going and the rivals are looking to put more pressure on the backs.

Something else, don't look at this as a short-yardage play. This is a potential big gainer. Don't use it on third and three. Use it on first and 10 or after a loss or penalty.

I can remember gaining 45 yards on this trap from the seven-yard line and against Concordia making 35 yards to dig us out of a hole.

There is nothing spectacular in the creation or function. Mainly, good timing. The quarterback gives the ball to the fullback and takes a bootleg sweep, pretending he has the ball on his hip. The center and right guard take care of the middle guard and the left guard pulls out to the right side.

I remember the sheer running ability of Cronin. He was not a fast man but he made many large gains off this play, veering to the right as he moved behind the double team block.

This is a great play for taking pressure off the passer. A beleagured quarterback welcomes the rest it gives. If he is hurt or tired, this play can give him time to recuperate.

Most of all, it makes heroes out of the blocking guards. These valuable fellows deserve all the pats on the back they can garner. They also prove to the running heroes how important the man up front is.

Like the day Knute Rockne put the Four Horsemen behind a patch-work line of subs and they were dropped consistently. He laughed and told the Horsemen, "Why don't you show them your clippings?"

Without the Seven Mules the Four Horsemen were just a good set of backs. With their Mules, they were immortals.

7
Coaching Underdogs and Favorites

Fortunately, I haven't been in the role of underdog much, but I have definite theories on that role. It goes back to continually mentioning to the squad why we should win and virtually ignoring the obvious advantages of the favorite.

This approach was illustrated candidly before our battle with Prairie View. This outfit had imposing specialists like Otis Taylor and Jim Kearny and others who would make prolific contributions in the NFL. Obviously they deserved to be rated a 10-point favorite. Their speed and specialists figured to strike often enough to beat our slower Johnnies. They were the national black champions. They had pulverized Grambling and run roughshod over the rest of the schedule. They were touted as one of the great small college teams of the decade.

We never let our team look at Prairie View films. I got a little frightened myself. They were capable of blinding us with their speed. I figured one look at them on film and my squad might develop a case of inferiority complex, regardless of what we have insisted all season; St. John's can't be beaten if it doesn't beat itself.

I couldn't prevent our players from reading the praise of Prairie View in the papers. But they would not see the speed on film. When a player would mention what the papers said about Prairie View's prowess, I would say, "Yes, they are good. I happen to think we are better."

I insisted we had secondary men who could keep up with their lightning—like receivers. I told our line that its rush could harass the passer. I told our team that we would hit longer, hit harder and use the chilly weather to good use. I said we were meant to weaken them by hammering and that their specialists wouldn't be able to stand up under the pounding. I probably knew deep down that I was whistling in a dark cemetery, but eventually I believed my own words.

That cold day we won a magnificent 33-27 shootout—and actually got as many spectacular plays from our forces as their hearlded specialists.

I have never played up the opposition. A newspaper man once said, "John, you can cry a lot about a lot of little things, but I never heard you tell your people the other team was better or had more talent." I'm glad he noticed, because I also have been accused of lamenting our lack of depth and lack of speed and vowing to use us for fodder. My team knows that I get out the crying towel before a lot of games, but they know it is a ploy and sometimes makes humorous copy. Maybe it sells a few tickets. I try to be as candid as possible. Sometimes, I suspect, my efforts at humor are misinterpreted. Like I've said, coaches could all use a good script writer.

What is serious is what I tell my team. They must know I believe we can win. They must know they are equipped with enough of an arsenal to win. They must know I have a plan I believe will win.

I recall playing a superior force of athletes with a struggling team. The other side supposedly had everything—the ground game and the aerial circus.

I told my players, "It's true they have exceptional balance—but I don't think they are ready for a few tricks. Let's put in three or four new ones and have some fun. Let's strike early and with deception. Lets put them back on their heels and keep them guessing. Let's show them that St. John's can do more things in a football game than just block and tackle."

We tried a little dipsy-do and the favorites actually panicked and worried more about our tricks than their own game. It was an easy upset. But was it an upset? I felt our team was better prepared mentally. We wanted to play a favorite. We were ready for the kill. It was the quiet mongoose going after the flashy cobra.

When we're the underdog, I stress that the first quarter is all important. If we get the first touchdown, we have a chance. If we get the first two, I doubt if they'll catch us. If we get the first three, it's all over.

Impact:

'When a 150-pounder creams a 200-pounder, I guess that's what they really mean when they talk of St. John's 'emotional impact.'

Conversely, I feel the same when we are the favorite, which we have been 80 percent of the time. I genuinely fear the first quarter. If the underdog rises up and scores first, we have a challenge. If he scores the first two times, it is suddenly an even game. If he scores three touchdowns without a return, we have suddenly become the underdog.

So there are two ways to approach the game depending on your role. As the underdog, we prepare for the quick strike. We want the other team off balance. If we create doubt, that can turn to eventual panic. And perhaps complete collapse. We will gamble more when we are the underdog. We will strive to exploit the long-gainer more often. We will hazard a few swashbuckling plays, making the other fellows ask, "Hey—what's this outfit trying to pull off?"

Famed coach Bear Bryant once said, "The most dangerous thing alive is an underdog with a big crowd that has just blocked a punt."

The favorite must be wily and anticipate the early big plays by the underdog. If you can puncture the underdog's emotional balloon in the first few minutes, it usually leads to a comfortable domination. If you give an underdog the early advantage you can expect to feel its fangs. When the underdog comes out on an emotional high jag, I continually stress putting it away fast. Nothing strokes emotional fires like early success.

ST. JOHN'S GRADUATE GENE McCARTHY, a former presidential candidate, takes time out from political chores to chat football with John in 1972.

Trying to regain control over an underdog which has capitalized on your early mistakes or over confidence is difficult and rare. In every "Anatomy of an Upset" there is a time when the favorite failed to capitalize on an obvious scoring situation.

I probably worry more about a two-touchdown underdog than I do about a foe of equal ability. First there is the tendency of your squad to naturally feel a shade over-confident. One time I put an unbeaten team's defensive unit down on the goal line looking at the rival's play from the 10-yard line for an hour. The squad asked "How come?" I said their mental attitude told me that they would be on the defensive deep in their territory all day.

The squad got the idea.

Sometimes something really drastic is needed. I recall Bernie Bierman, a coach of legendary stature at the University of Minnesota, calling off drills two days before a Wisconsin game explaining, "It's obvious you fellows aren't this serious about the Badgers. I hope you remember to show up Saturday." The Gophers showed up and walloped their ancient foes.

I recall the story of Knute Rockne stopping drills one day before a game in which the Irish were natural favorites. He threw out a batch of newspapers on the field and told the squad, "Here, fellows, read the headlines about how good you are. Apparently you don't think you need the practice." The next game they won by four touchdowns.

I had a player ask me one time, "John, how come we practice as hard before the easy games as the tough ones?" I had to smile. I finally said, "What's an easy game? I never had one in 25 years of coaching. If you mean the game we won by a larger margin. Well, they weren't easier. We practice harder to win."

I recall that a few years ago a feisty Bethel team in St. Paul nearly knocked us off and I'm sure we were rated at least 30-point favorites. I am now in the process of getting together clips of that game and other games where we were prohibitive favorites. Players are impressed by what they see on films.

Upsets are part of the game. Vince Lombardi epitomized how we feel at St. John's about being the favorite and getting knocked off: "Green Bay is never upset. Now and then time runs out."

It is a difficult challenge to prepare for the underdog. First, you must drain the complacency of your team. That is a natural aura. Then you must work that much harder to prepare for the rivals' tricks and quick strikes—the same ones you would devise to use in their situation. It is particularly difficult when you come off a major victory against a traditional rival and move into the den of the snarling, ambitious underdog. This just might be the most difficult coaching situation a leader finds himself in.

That happened to me years ago. We beat a traditional rival by 20 points and had to come back and play a cellar team that hadn't beaten us for over five years.

The team must have thought I was crazy when I installed three new plays, dressed up some other sets, worked them harder and longer, and stressed timing and precision more than I had done in any other drills. I could feel resentment building even though we don't work that hard physically. I was demanding concentration when the situation seemed to call for some fun and levity.

Halfway through drills I called the team around me. I asked, "Do you men realize how often a team wins one big game and gets upset the next week by a so-called nothing? Well, I've been looking at this for years and we will be clay pigeons, prime targets this week. We can't be off our game even 10 percent because those other guys are going to be playing 50 percent better than they know how. We have to forget last week. The real test is this week."

I was right. It was a savage, tough, punishing encounter. We won by a touchdown in the last few minutes. We needed our new plays and we needed every ounce of concentration we could muster. You don't face the underdog after a big win unless you're ready for the battle of your life.

I point out that even in the ranks of the pros, underdogs can win about 47 percent of the time. I tell our young men if the best in the business can continually be upset, then we, certainly, are prone to being upset. But again, I emphasize that we are good enough to overcome whatever the underdog throws at us. I don't preach out of fear. I coach out of preparedness. I tell my players that regardless of how keyed the other team may be, the St. John's way will win. But if we are not playing up to our potential and if we make even a few mistakes, we are prone and vulnerable because of ourselves, not the rivals hype.

The mental aspect, the concentration, the willingness to believe— that's what a successful coach must instill. There is never a way of telling what is going on in the minds and bodies of 50 young men. I recall Knute Rockne saying to his team: "I have given you the physical and mental preparations. You are ready for the game of your lives. But I have no idea what's in your hearts. That's up to you to show me."

There are many coaches for whom I anguish who will be in the unfortunate position of underdogs most of their careers. God, what a challenge they face in schools with under-manned personnel, little tradition and no success on which to build. They are truly to be admired. Each Saturday they must re-convince their charges they have a chance. The giant-killer must live only to prey—not to forget dynasties. These are the great men in our profession—the ones who rarely make the headlines and who must compensate for lack of talent consistently by building from the spirit and heart.

An old coaching friend who played as the underdog for years said, "It's a magnificent way of making a living. I'm a hero when we do what we're not supposed to—win."

Bob Zuppke, an old master, said that the fury of a raging underdog equaled that of a tigeress cornered.

My motto has always been: Respect the underdog but don't play into his hands.

And when going against a top heavy favorite I have always insisted: Gamble like a riverboat card player, get there fast and hope they panic.

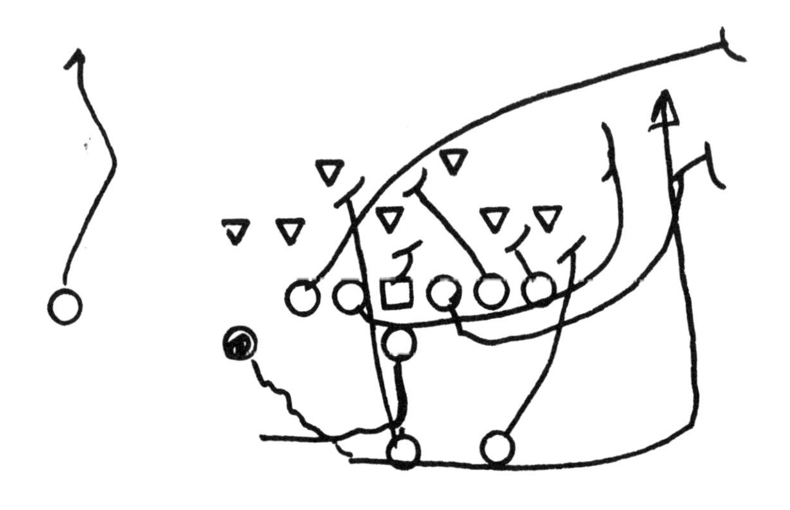

A Pleasant Embarrassment

Another power sweep, which may not be as spectacular as the one with the tackle pulling, but which is more like a mud-slide: you don't know the damage until you try to clean up the house.

We have run this sweep so many years and so many times, it is embarrassing. But there is nothing to make us red-faced about the statistics. It has averaged 5.9 over the years—almost six yards per carry. Considering every foe sets out to bottle up this play, I think the figures are remarkable.

I think more than anything else, they reflect the players' confidence in a play that has served us well for over 30 years. You simply get out and knock people over and get the running back around the corner. I tell them I want to see them come off the corner like A. J. Foyt, the race driver; hard and fast and clean.

I remember Lou Raiola leading the conference in rushing and I'll wager nearly half of it came off this play. Behind the wave of blockers, Lou ran with high-kneed optimism and confidence. It usually took two or three tacklers to bring him down. On our 1976 championship team, Jim Roeder and Scott Edstrom were highly effective.

As you can see the quarterback comes away from the center and begins a move left, handing to the running block going right. The play can move to either side, but the quarterback fake after the give is vitally important. That gives the back just that second edge to move against the grain of the defense. Both guards are pulling, the left end cuts right downfield for more blocking and one running back fakes into the line before the handoff.

The right side of the defense has to ponder the back coming into the line or the quarterback going outside. By the time the sweeping back has his three to four men wave of blockers and the momentum, it can be an awesome amount of offensive muscles.

I like to think of it as a World War II convoy with massed protection for the supply ship—which happens to be the runner.

Rivals have called it "The St. John's Tornado" and "The St. John's Army March" and "The St. John's Assault Force." It is simple, functional and should work on any field but preferably a dry one with solid footing.

If a rival can't stop this sweep, it is in serious trouble against St. John's. This is a big damage play. I recall one coach who had tried to stop it all afternoon, saying: "St. John's could have beaten us with the one play."

I remember Billy Conn trying to slug it out with Joe Louis in the thirteenth round of their dramatic heavyweight title fight. Afterwards they asked Billy what punch put him away. "When you're hit by Joe you don't remember which punch." I think it's that way with this power sweep. It kind of grinds you down. You may stop it now and then, but after the game is over, you usually find it has been used nearly a dozen times and has piled up heavy yardage.

It is a particularly wearing play on lighter secondary backs who must consistently throw themselves into the flow. They have a feeling as the game progresses that maybe they are caught in some kind of meat grinder.

The runners like it because it gives them the feeling of power and massed forces at their command. The sheer exhilaration of running behind three or four fast-moving blockers pumps confidence and adrenalin into most backers.

Momentum on this play is everything. It is geared to work like a runaway freight, developing sweep and power as it goes.

If I had one play I would pick out of our book which I believe has served us best over the years, this just might be it.

By the way, I look at this play as an off-shoot of the old single wing, a formation I loved. You'll have old-timers in the stands who recall the old hoary single wing plays of yesterday with massed blocking and waves of assualt troops. It has had nice ink in the papers and, like I've said, it's becoming a virtual tradition of St. John's as much as monks chanting.

THE LAST WORDS BEFORE KICKOFF sometimes are the most important game preparation of all at St. John's.

A SOLITARY MOMENT between the coach and his quarterback.

8
Deciding On the Nature of the Beast

Any coach who decides early on in his career that he will win on power or stress just passing or will fit the cogs to a new formation, I feel is making a grave mistake. We decide what kind of team we'll be only after I decide who is going to be quarterback. This position wills the type of outfit I will try to mould.

For instance, Jeff Norman and my son, John, were option quarterbacks and we naturally stressed the option. If we had passing quarterbacks like Gary Marlow, Mike Kozlak and John Welsch along with sure-handed receivers, we went to the passing game. We knew receivers like John Hanowski, Mike Grant, Dave Arnold and Todd Watson would make a passing attack the prime weapon.

Now, with a great running back like Tom Wagner, we build an offense around him. The idea was to get the ball to him as much as possible. The same with men I've coached like John Balestri, Rich Froehle and Tim Schmidt: men who were so durable and had so much stamina they could carry a team on the ground.

In 1983 I had a fine thrower in Denny Schlepper and a great runner in Ricky Bell, so we were pretty much a 50-50 football team, although because of Bell's receiving we leaned toward the more wide-open style of play.

Ultimately the quarterback is the man who shapes the team for me. In our system, you must understand, the quarterback calls the plays 90 percent of the time. They tell me only about 20 percent of the teams today let the quarterback call his own signals. I love this technique. I have always felt strongly that we are teaching college players leadership and the ability to make quick decisions. I think of a coach as a drama teacher. If he or she is doing the job well, the actors can stand on their own two feet. If we are truly educators, then we should strive to give the team and that quarterback the sense of confidence to do it on his own.

How else will they learn to cope with life's problems and appraise life's values? Besides, I never knew a quarterback who honestly wouldn't prefer to make his own calls. It's a rewarding experience. Plus, the quarterback has the feel of the game, his instincts on the field can sense even better than a sideline strategist the tempo, the ebb and flow of the action. That's why he wants to play quarterback—to utilize his instincts and generalship.

Our quarterbacks seem to relish this system and thrive on it. Oh yes, we can make mistakes. But what about the ones the coaches make? I think my record speaks for my theories on quarterbacks. I place my faith in them.

Of course, game strategy isn't left all to the quarterback's judgment. We have a game play—a detailed design conceived during practice. But he has optional attack routes and we value his suggestions during the heat of battle. In one perplexing situation near a rival's goal line, the quarterback asked me what I thought. I put my arm around him and told him, "You got us 80 yards—you must have an idea how to get into the end zone." He had an idea, we used it and scored on the next play. Too often coaches place so much faith in men stationed all over the stadium, operating through a complicated network of electronics and intricate signal systems.

I, of course, use none of these. I love the feel of the game the quarterback is sensing. I love to utilize his instincts. I can't believe men six stories up in a press box can feel the same thing or sense the arousal or emotional sag that the men on the field can.

One of the few advantages a coach on the sidelines or upstairs may have is watching the point of attack and see perhaps more clearly why a play may have failed. But, in general, I think the quarterback is the instrument which should ignite the play. If he is not comfortable with an option, he is not as likely to call it. If he is not a polished passer, he won't pass that much. I have found my quarterbacks think with calculations based on their ability to get the play functioning. I believe they can sense the time for the "kill" and the time for control better than anyone along the sidelines.

Of course, on one out of every five or six plays I suggest, something because, perhaps, I have seen a defensive adjustment the quarterback might not have been in a position to see. There have been times when my quarterbacks did not feel they could function at top capacity while worrying about the plays. Then I am perfectly willing to send in the plays. But we try to instill in our players that St. John's teaches leadership. We point to senators, bankers, leaders in all phases of industry, and tell them, "You can develop a lot of these traits of greatness by deciding how to call a football game." Even coaching high school, I let my quarterbacks call the majority of our plays.

I do stress in our play-calling that we strive for the unexpected—we have always in the St. John's way tried to keep the foe off balance. If he looks for the run—throw. If he looks for the pass—run. It's the same as the hitter and pitcher in baseball. The pitcher tries to outguess the batter with either a fast ball, curve, slider or change-up. We have short runs, long-gain hopefuls, short passes, bombs and a few gimmicks.

I remember a coach saying to me after our team had scored six touchdowns on plays that caught his outfit completely off guard, "You didn't overpower us today, anyway, John. But you sure tricked the hell out of us." Not really tricks. We rarely had passes on first down, but in this particular game we passed seven times on first down against a defense stacked heavily against the run. I had remembered the previous year the same coach saying after we averaged 5.5 yards running on first down, "I know one thing...The Johnnies will never run us into the ground again on first down." I figured this as the time to throw.

Getting back to the style of teams, I have absolutely no preconceived idea of what type of team we will be until drills begin. I've had quarterbacks get injured in the off season and have to redesign our plans. I've had newcomers take away quarterbacks' starting jobs and bring us an entirely new set of gifts.

Never, I urge young coaches, should you be so moulded in theory and concept that you try to make a quarterback or any key player be something he is not, just for the sake of your preconceived plans. Plans are easy to change. Quarterbacks are not.

Getting back to first down passes for a moment, I never really relished them over the years. But I had a splendid passer in Gary Marlowe who asked me; "Do you have any preference in first down plays? I mean can I pass?" I thought for a moment, and something seemed to tell me this young man had irrepressible confidence in his ability to throw on first down. I let him loose. He completed four of his first five passes on first down situations for nearly 100 yards.

I looked at the figures. Our quarterback is usually matching wits with the other coach and we're winning about 75 percent of the time. I think that should answer the question: Can quarterbacks call their own games?

Let's look at it another way. All plays are designed to gain yards. Really, the quarterback can't possible call a bad play. Any play you give him in the game plan is designed to move forward. He might choose a play too risky for the given situation. Then again, maybe it will catch the defense completely flat-footed. How can we possible not let him have the chance?

One year we had a fourth down and six-inch situation on the rival's 30-yard line. I would have called a straight ahead smash. Instead the quarterback, my son John, faked a dive play to the fullback and lofted a soft lob pass to a receiver who had drifted behind the line of scrimmage just six yards down field. He scored untouched, again proving that the man on the field knows best most of the time.

Position:

"I've never guaranteed a player a position. In my system a 170-pound breakaway with a gazelle's speed might wind up a pull-out guard. I can promise them excitement."

I do believe quarterbacks calling their own plays will use a few more high-risk calls than the ones a coach might send in from the bench. But then I ask myself, if his plays fools me, why shouldn't it fool the opposition?

For years the other coaches in our conference called the Johnnies' football "mash-mouth" style. That's because for several years we had featured grinding power games. But then, too, our passing statistics have always been among the league's best. Naturally I've been asked at clinics and informal gatherings, "Just what kind of a coach are you?"

The nature of the beast is difficult to define. Passing and winning must complement each other. It would be impossible to run 60 times and pass 60 times. When they refer to my mash-mouth what they are really saying is that I don't have the talented option quarterback I need for a balance assault. Then I rely on strong blocking and less on finesse. I have developed a solid "ride" series, which many young coaches have honored me by using. St. Thomas College's fine young staff has stated openly that they take a few of our plays each year and absorb them in their system. That makes me feel proud.

Now this ride series can be a consistent gainer, but I must have the right type of quarterback to make it work with telling effect. We run when we think we have the quarterback for it: the man with the right instincts for when to run, when to hand-off, when to pitch, a quick thinker with good hands and worlds of confidence.

If you looked at our statistics over the years, you'd have trouble quessing our pattern. Two years ago we stumbled with an all-out air arm. Next year I vowed that we would balance off the air on the ground. There are times when a young quarterback can dazzle you in drills and you are ready to move a mountain to entertain his gifts. But in the game he tightens and the offense freezes.

Letting a quarterback stamp your attack is not always easy. You must be certain what you see in drills is what you'll get in a game. Like boxers, some quarterbacks—passers in particular—are sensational in the gym, but when the bell rings they can come apart at the seams.

I remember Coach Royal at Texas always saying he "would dance with the girl I brought to party." Meaning his ground games got him to the big games and the bowls and he figured they would keep him winning. But I still love the theory "Keep 'em guessing." Nobody can throw an ambush if they don't know when the wagons are going through the pass.

It gets down to building an attack that cannot be outguessed; building it around a quarterback or a slashing runner who performs at or close to maximum capabilities at all times. I have never had the luxury of going out and hand-picking a grade A, blue-chip quarterback sought by many. I have to make use of the talent that shows up. I'm not complaining. Some of my walk-ons have turned out beautifully. We don't get any prep all-Americans, but we get young men who want to think, who want to improve and who want to test their ingenuity and intelligence and judgment in tough situations.

I'll take that kind of quarterback.

And on his ability we'll define the nature of the beast.

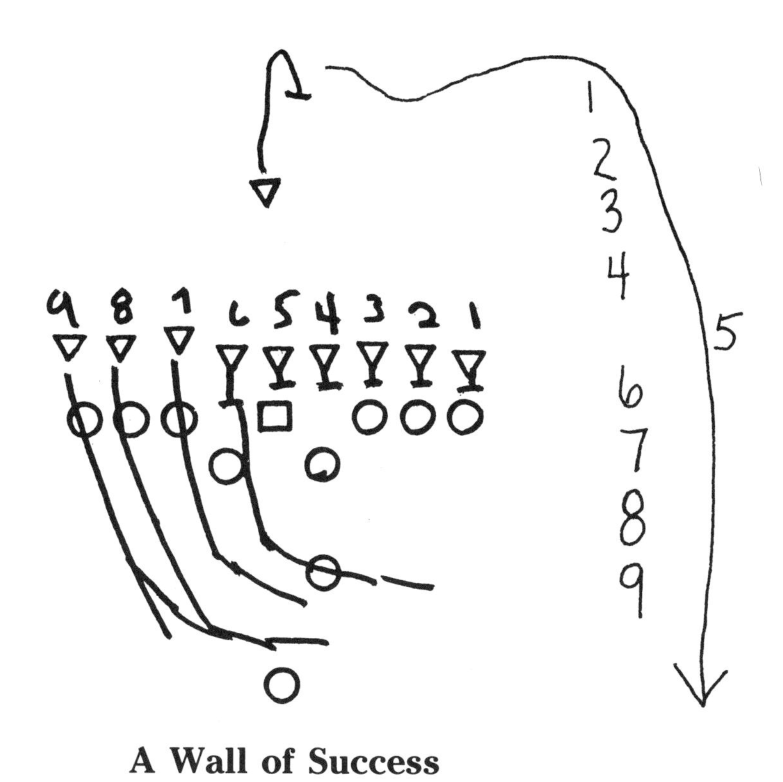

A Wall of Success

The St. John's punt return has created a wall of success for us over the years. One season we actually averaged close to 18 yards per turn, which had to place us among the nation's leaders. In the mid-1950s we had particular success. Fleet Tom (Whizzer) White ran back five of them for tremendous yardage in the first half against the University of Duluth in one game, piling up over 180 yards.

And how about Bob Spinner piling up heavy yardage with the punt return and turning the tide against St. Thomas College one game with his great broken-field running behind alert blocking? He got us into the national championship battle with Prairie View.

Another great punt-return hero was Jerry Haugen. Little Bill Laliberte was a mere speck among giants, but he found ways to slither through the special teams with superb punt returns.

Perhaps none of them equaled Joe Luby, who might have been the all-time St. John's punt-return hero with many dazzling runs on the 1976 national championship team. He never made a fair catch and he ran back seven for touchdowns during his career, averaging over 55 yards on the scoring runs.

Punt returns can change the complexion of games. They can take the heart out of good teams. No one play, save perhaps an interception, can do so much to switch the tide of a battle.

I recall St. John's was losing by three touchdowns in the third quarter on a

A SPEAKER IN CONSTANT DEMAND, John charms large audiences all over the Midwest.

FATHER HILLARY speaks eloquently of John's deeds at the 1983 testimonial. Agreeing in the the background is Dorothy Riley.

rainy, gloomy day and I felt we had lost the momentum. Suddenly, a dramatic 88-yard punt return inflamed our forces to such a degree that we became virtually unstoppable. The good punt return works for you from a strategic, territorial and psychological way to take the confidence out of a foe.

It is a magnificent opportunity to put rekindled desire into your team. Our average on punt and kickoff returns has always been excellent. I tell the men, "This is a chance to show your extemporaneous ability—your talent for doing things on the spot; for making up the moves that can become a game-breaker. In no other offensive play is the player so much a part of creating the result. He has to have instinct to feel where the openings may arise—where there is a seam that seems to be opening or a wall that appears to be setting up. It calls for very great creative instinct by the ball carrier. Once into the open field he must move in such a way that his blockers are in a good position to wipe out remaining tacklers. He, at times, will find he must pause and wait for blockers to catch up or regroup.

As you see in the play, I designate numbers to the linemen and then approximate where they should be on the return. In this diagram, the right side of the line is putting on the rush and the left side falls back to form the wall with the rushing men eventually moving along the wall near the sidelines. The runner will try to hide or maneuver behind that wall. But he always has the alternative of breaking out and going against the grain if he feels he is being pressured out of bounds.

One year we averaged over 20 yards on the returns we were able to run back. I credit the linemen in visually being able to imagine a wall and spacing themselves the four or five yards apart to make a corridor.

There is nothing technical about this play. The runner seeks the wall and the blockers attempt to create a corridor between the foe and the sidelines. It is a thing of beauty when properly executed because no play has all the men moving farther to set up the blocking pattern. It calls for smart, mobile linemen. They must realize again that they will get little applause.

The ball carrier is the hero. So what is new?

9

Control vs. Lightning and Gimmickry

Put a gun to my head, back me into a corner and demand to know which I prefer most, ball control or the fast strike—and I'd probably have to say, "the long gainers." Or, as I love to call 'em "heart-breakers."

I guess I prefer to win, if I can, with the long gainers, the overland express. Don't get me wrong. If ball control is what my team does best, then ball control it is. But I have a love affair with the quick-strike attack, the kind that can immobilize a defense in seconds and have its men asking,"Which way did they go?"

I once had a friend at a coaching clinic argue that ball control is the only thing. It prevents, he said, the rival from doing that much damage. But, by the same token, the longer you have the ball the more opportunities for mistakes. How many faultless 75-yard, 15-play drives can you recall last season?

Something else: I greatly admire the ball control of a winning high school team, and while it is in the lead and not making mistakes, it is virtually impossible to beat. But when it finds itself behind late in the game, it still has to grind it out, chug for the four or five yards and has lost a lot of playoff games because it can't strike from behind. It needs five or six or seven minutes to make things happen. Ball control teams are terrific front runners. They also can be awkward when you need points in a hurry. The long-gainers, the heart-breakers are difficult to suddenly embrace in the offensive plan when you've been thinking four-yards-per-crack.

When we have the right quarterback, we can play high-risk football and I don't actually consider it risky. We have played it as wide-open as any team in the country. Instead of high risk, we think of our distance, quick strikes as surprises. For instance, on one play we can choose any of five options and two passes. But this kind of attack demands the right man as quarterback.

I just hope that I never hear that a team can "read" St. John's. I'd love to know when the other team thinks it knows Gagliardi. We can change course and strategy in seconds. I have always admired the generals and leaders who are willing to deviate from the obvious. Of course we have game plans, but they are subject to change—sometimes on a whim. The one correlation that remains secure through all this is the belief that whatever we try will work. Again, complete, almost blind faith in the St. John's way.

It's healthy to switch offenses in midstream. It gives the psyche an airing. It is emotionally stimulating to try something new. We may have complete success with ball control and then, on perhaps the fourth or fifth possession of the ball, drop in something completely and wondrously new. Remember, I said stay with the offense that is working and winning. But that is no reason not to complement the dimensions and scope of your offensive with new, fun plays every now and then. That way, when you are behind and need to strike quickly, you have complete faith in the new wrinkle.

I call it being adjustable—being able to live with new things. Haven't you regularly seen a team try a new play and it backfires so badly that the team looks so inept you have pity? You know the coach won't try that again for a decade.

Charting what we like to call the "unthinkables," we have found out that they work nearly 55 percent of the time for major gains the first time we use them. Anything that works 44 percent of the time for a distance gain certainly can be used when you need that late rally or the fusillade as the seconds run down.

I have heard major coaches argue against the so-called gimmicks. Yet, a surprising number of old but always new statue of liberty and flea-flicker plays even stun the professionals. There is nothing wrong with the wrinkle play if you believe in it. The trouble with gimmicks is that they are usually on the spectacular side, naked almost in their excecution to the point where everybody in the stadium suddenly realizes what you are trying to do. Consequently, when they don't work, it is easy to spot a goat or label the coach a screwball.

Thrills:

"No greater thrill for me than watching a little football player chop down the big man. That little man will never forget the feeling through life...he'll always love to take a shot at the big odds."

People sometimes forget that Bernie Bierman, whose dreadnaughts at Minnesota were the symbol of power at its zenith, used the buck-lateral series with devastating effectiveness and many times lateraled off forward passes. The lateral, although sparingly used, was always in the repertoire of the Grey Eagle and used enough so that the Gophers were never shaky when it was called.

It's a wonderful feeling of elation and it still gives me goosebumps to stand watching practice during a beautiful fall day and suddenly conjure up a play out of our ordinary pattern—something that might startle the foe and perhaps even break open a tight game. I like to think of myself as a man for any season. And please don't laugh, but I have some plays where we have ends and even centers carrying the ball—and even throwing it. The trouble is, if everything is going right, we have a tendency to forget them during the game.

But I like to believe every coach has a little artist in him. One double reverse and forward pass with a lateral tacked on can be a piece of art by the very fact the defense is so bewildered at the inception and conclusion you know his whole game plan has to suffer. Meanwhile, you have told your team, "Hey, we are smarter than these fellows. We tricked 'em!" A gimmick play has righted many sinking ships.

In over 30 years of coaching, I guess we have won perhaps seven or eight games on pure gimmickry and the use of the trickster has probably got us back into maybe a dozen games. That's not a great percentage but the enjoyment to the team can't be measured. Players will meet years later and talk about the time the tackle-eligible romped 40 yards.

Don't turn your back on the gimmick and say, "Gosh, time doesn't permit us even to get our basic stuff polished." That's a cop-out. The wrinkle plays can break the monotony for the players and hype their enthusiasm. Even if you only use them in drills, they serve the purpose of making the game more enjoyable.

While talking about this, I will vow right now to use more tricks next season. The longer I think about it, why not? The players love the excitement. The element of surprise is worth a twelfth player on the field.

There are critics who say only bad teams resort to gimmick plays. But I tell them, remember Knute Rockne. He switched jerseys on his backs in practices one time to fool the media enroute to a Southern California game which nobody expected the Irish to win. On the first possession he juggled the backs and because the Trojans thought a certain star was plagued by injuries, over-shifted one way while the Notre Dame surprise sprinter raced another and before it was over Rockne had won by a rout. He explained, "Sometimes when the muscle isn't there you must make the head do the job." That holds true today.

Don't laugh, but some day I hope to score on the hidden ball trick. And I am determined that some day my center will get loose on a 50-yard run.

I am serious when I say the element of surprise is worth a twelfth man. In one game we reversed on a kickoff and threw a lateral for good measure. The play gained 68 yards. Another time we tacked three laterals on the end of a pass and gained over 50 yards. I have had punters pass and punters run and lateral. I have used a double reverse on a punt return. Sometimes a rival spends so much time worrying about its fundamentals that it is completely shocked by anything out of the ordinary. I try to catalogue in my brain how our opposition thinks and plans. This can be foolish at times because any plan will work if the machine is functioning. It is still execution and timing. But there are some teams whose dimensions are narrow enough so that an early trick play will throw a defense in disarray. Intense, pressuring defenses need to be dealt with by surprise. There are times to match muscle — and times to scoot around the wall or drop behind it.

Your team must have such faith in the system and the salesman running it that it makes no difference where the long-gainers are launched. I have tried wild, high-risk plays on our 15-yard line. I have tried the same ones on the rival's 15. I find that they work about half the time either place. It is the faking and ball handling; the look of the passer one way and the throw another direction. I find that gimmick plays usually backfire for the simple reason they aren't used enough. So give it a whirl in scrimmage. Wind up the day's drill with half a dozen fun plays. Lord, if the game can't be fun, we shouldn't be playing it. I sometimes think the major schools take it all to seriously.

That's why I was so delighted when Joe Kapp's California outfit used six laterals and ran through the Stanford band on the last play to win a traditional battle. I have to believe right this moment that Joe is sketching a couple of more dipsy-do wonders to shock the Pacific Coast.

Sometimes you have to sell your own club on the long-bomb trick. I had a running back who didn't throw the ball five times in high school. He didn't believe he was capable of catching a 15-yard lateral pass across the field from the quarterback, spotting a receiver, getting the feel of the ball and throwing it 30 yards.

He complained, "John, I think you're making a big mistake." I didn't put any pressure on him. I just said, "Maybe I'm wrong and things will never work. But I know one thing, if you can get the ball out there in the direction of the receiver, he's good enough to catch it. I don't care if the pass looks like a sack of grain going through a wind tunnel — just get it up and out."

He laughed and said, "OK, but you won't be sore if it backfires." I said, "Heck, have fun."

Well, the first time we tried it the receiver was wide open and he threw the ball almost into the concession stands. He was off target by 20 yards. But he came back to the quarterback and said, "Gimme another chance. I was just nervous." In the next quarter he fired a perfect spiral for a 37-yard gain. He repeated it three more times that year. At the football dinner, he joshed me, "John, if you were really smart, you'd have seen my passing potential from the start."

Passing is confidence. The gimmick play is confidence. Getting the long, trick play or the new wrinkle to work means you again rely on salesmanship. Don't approach it with the idea this is life and death and that it means the Seventh Game of a World Series. It should be fun. It should be a challenge. It should work if your own team is not afraid of it. Rivals don't kill off gimmickry. The operating team usually does itself in. It has everything going for it: the surprise element, usually the timing, the newness and the fact the opposition has not been working against it.

Control football can be a joy. It is a safety first — backed by the insurance companies of the globe. I have loved our mash-mouth clubs that could hardly wait to take the ball on our 20-yard line with six minutes to play, trailing. They would always say to me, "Don't worry. All the time in the world. We should take it with 20 seconds to spare." And how often I have seen them come through. Again, a figure I am so proud of: coming from behind in the last half of the fourth quarter to win nearly 30 percent of our victories!

Short, controlled passing always has been a forte with these teams. Just enough passing to keep the linebackers off our runners' necks. I have had teams which were so sure of their ability to execute 80-yard marches, you could almost set your watches by the time they would reach mid-field and then the foe's 20. But these teams had the two or three or four little surprises if they needed them. I think it is unfair to harness a ball control power team solely with the block-and-gouge routine. I have always said there is nothing more beautiful in football than massed blocking getting down field six and seven yards ahead of a churning fullback who suddenly is in the open spaces.

But there have been times when good power units ran out of clock. There have been times when horrendous November fields in blustery Minnesota shackled out best runners in quagmire and mud and snow and sleet and ice. That is why a team must always have something left in its arsenal, so that it can reach down and bring up the unexpected.

Here is where I'd like to bring up a thought and fact that may surprise you. Everybody in football lore called Bronko Nagurski the hardest runner, strongest runner and greatest plunger in pro football infancy. "Give the ball to the Bronk" became a battle cry of the old Chicago Bears. What people forget is that Nagurski also could pass and had the highest passing percentage in the club. Even Nag knew that he couldn't run through an 11-man defense continually, particularly in goal-line stance. So he became proficient at the take-and-jump pass, the soft lob over the line. George Halas always said, "Nag could do everything — including pass."

Let there be a mighty lesson gained here. If the greatest line-cracker in history still deemed it necessary at times to throw the ball and use a little trickery, it professes how important the change-of-pace play is.

You may have the world's greatest collection of muscles and a 270-pound line moving like mass snowplows, but there will come a time when the funny little gismo play is the most explosive weapon you own.

Practice it. Play with it. Have fun with it. Best of all, don't fear making up a zany little trick and exploit the foe's surprise. Sometimes the play you draw up for laughs brings tears to the enemy.

Oh yes, I constantly am asked what is the best scoring play inside the 15-yard line. I have a ready answer: the play-action pass. It doesn't require a great thrower but it requires almost perfect defensive execution to stop the play. Run a receiver deep one way, let the quarterback also fake that same direction and hit the receiver who usually has one-on-one coverage. If the receiver has a problem, the quarterback generally can get close or get in by faking the pass with good throwing motion.

If I had one play to work on all week, this is the one I'd polish. Checking back over the last decade, I believe we have scored nearly 30 percent on this type of play. The execution is simple and fun. Defensively, it provides the secondary with two choices — come up or cover — all done in a split second with only two or three seconds of running needed to reach the double stripe. The fake in the opposite direction holds linebackers and must be done with camouflage and sleight-of-hand that any good quarterback can master. If he has a little speed, so much the more effective.

A smart defensive coach told me, "If I could eliminate one play from book inside the 30, it would be the play-action pass or run. It's a killer on defenses because, operated properly, there is virtually no defense."

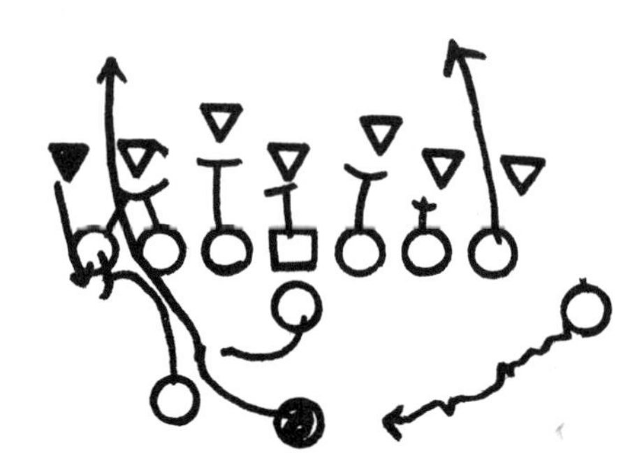

'Mash-Mouth Football'

When all else fails, I tell my team we are going to "Mash-Mouth" football. It's becoming a standing joke with all St. John's teams. There are days, I point out, when trickery will get you nothing. There are days when passes backfire like boomerangs. There are days when punt return men fumble and quarterbacks forget plays. But good old Mash-Mouth is always on hand. It seems to return things to normal.

Maybe the field is miserable and you can't get decent footing to turn the corner. Maybe the field is frozen and the light-horse cavalry can't run and the quarterback's fingers are numb. Mash-Mouth football to the rescue!

This play epitomizes inside football at its best. We return to it so often. It is a core to ground game supremacy. I recall a game where this play set a standard by which I was to judge all future Johnny inside attacks.

We were playing a typically talented, strong Concordia team coached by the great Jake Christiansen in 1963. Jake moved in his best and one of his most powerful defensive men to counter this play. We didn't know it but we would be running right into the teeth of the man who would go on to become a pro football star at 250 pounds.

Anyway, Bernie Beckman at 155 pounds was assigned to take out this mighty defensive end. This was a championship game and the stakes were high. But Bernie actually handled his massive and active foe many times during the afternoon enroute to our 28-0 victory.

I always remember this game. I always remember saying that now I believe a good, little man, functioning with skill and desire, can handle a giant foe. Beckman was unbelievable that day.

As you can see on the diagram, the runner takes the handoff and behind a double-team block on the defensive tackle and the other running back getting the end, we were heading a heavy assault to the left side. Of course, we change blocking assignments, but it is basically the same play over the years, run perhaps eight to 15 times a game, depending on the defense and the situation.

Besides the strong blocking, we have had players who love to run the simple Mash-Mouth play. Tom Wagner, Rich Froehle, Joe Cronin, Jon Balestri, Ricky Bell, Tim Schmitz, the Eustices — Gary and Brad — I could go on with a litany of power-runners who loved this play.

Once into a secondary, they were pretty much on their own. Our blockers' primary objective is to get the man into the secondary and then let him use his speed and power. The play is designed for five or six yards. It has averaged as much as 8.4 in championship games.

This is a great muddy field play. Against Gustavus Adolphus in 1982 we ran it 26 times and Ricky Bell piled up most of his 135 yards with it.

The simplicity perhaps is what adds to it. It appears easy to top. But it is a challenge to the blockers to make the clean hits and it is a challenge to the runners to hit the hole at the split second it opens. We have been fortunate that our players over the years have enjoyed the play to the extent it almost lets them say to the rivals, "Well, here we go again with the old workhorse. Nothing fancy — but try to stop it."

Blockers who come to mind because they loved this play and the nose-to-nose action it created are Rich Chalmers, Denny Sharkey, John Sowada, Sev Youso and John McDowell and Hammer Kramer. These were young men who prided themselves in tough, furious scrimmage action. They loved the contact in the pits.

I love this play. It has set the table for the other plays so often. It has given our team pride: pride to know they could make a simple, power thrust work on sheer execution and bulldog tenacity. It is a Mash-Mouth play that requires the complete faith by the players.

Mash-Mouth plays like these will never go out of style. They are what rock-sock, hard-gut football is all about.

10
The Theories of Defense

Philosopher and educator Charles Simmons once said the "weakest spot in mankind is where they fancy themselves most wise and strong."

I have always looked at our defense before the season started and thought of those words. If I felt we really had a solid pass defense corps, I say, "Hey — don't get complacent. Here is where we really need to work." If I felt in my heart our pass rush would be excellent, I'd remember Simmons' words. This is where the Achilles heel could develop. If I thought our linebacking array was ready for a great season, I'd caution myself and say, "Let's get back to the drawing board and work harder on the linebacking."

How often have you heard it said at the end of a losing year, "Gosh this was the year we expected our end play to be the best. Instead, it really fell apart." Or "I can't figure out how bad our tackles and nose-guards play. I really thought we'd be a whale of a team up front but injuries hurt and we lost heart."

What I am driving at is this: I have to believe coaches should approach defensive planning by expecting the worst. I don't mean to sound like a pessimist. Heaven forbid! But defensively I find you can't count for certain on anything. If you do, you are in serious trouble.

I have counted on having exceptional special teams — only to face complete faceliftings as the season progresses. I have counted on safety men being leaders but have had to install new faces. Defense offers a constant challenge — just as creating and polishing a defense.

Unlike larger schools, some of which have enough assistants to let them actively run the defense, I have had to keep my hands in all phases of the game. Every defense has a distinct personality. Cultivate it like you would a rare plant. Nurture weaknesses and never forget: leaks usually develop where you least expect it.

In 1963 I was so proud we led the nation in rushing defense, limiting the opposition to just 12.9 yards per game!

But I have had teams that gave up 120 yards a game along the ground and were winners. I have had teams that give up 2.2 points per game to lead statistical categories and teams that still won titles giving up 20 points per game.

Like I have emphasized to other coaches, every defense has its own particular character traits. I have had teams that gave up ground rather easily until the foe got inside our 20 — then just as if somebody had pushed a button, they became savage defenders when their territory was threatened. They inevitably came up with the big play deep in our territory. Proud men, but difficult on a coach.

I have had other teams that always made one big play — either a quarterback sack — or an interception or the blocked punt. I have always believed that a blocked punt or a pass interception does more to destroy a rival's morale than anything outside of a losing fumble on the goal line.

So I don't try to develop a "type" of defense. I try to create 11 men on a defensive platoon who are comfortable in their positions, work as a unit and keep thinking "big play." I once told a defensive crew, "Our offense may sputter this year and I expect you fellows to supply some points." They brought us directly or indirectly 11 touchdowns on vital defensive plays near the enemy goal line.

You have teams that I call, "Human sponges." Ours last year was a lot like that. It would give us ground and then, seemingly, when it was in serious trouble, make the game breaking play. There are defensive teams that lay back and soak up the foe, never letting them have the big gain but making the coach sweat by permitting themselves to be chewed up a little along the way. There are the attack defenses which find themselves trapped at times, by-passed at times and fooled horribly on occasion. But these also have the ability to force mistakes, keep on constant, irrepressible pressure; get hand-on hand-off or bat a pitch-out of control. They can be fooled and look absolutely horrible — but have a knack of tenacity and ball-hawking which eventually disrupts the rival's entire game plan.

I believe basically in the five-man line. But I am not ignoring the sophisticated passing of today's game and the need for dropping back more linemen in aerial coverage. We were using what they call the three-man line as early as 1960. Only then we called it the end-drop-off.

Injuries:

"Nothing pains me as much as to visit an injured football player in the hospital room. Somehow, I always feel responsible for their pains."

We created what they called the "Monster" back in 1954 when we had a rugged, aggressive two-way combative player named Dick Miller who weighed 215 pounds and had an excellent start. We didn't know quite where to play him on defense so we made him an additional outside linebacker or a double end. He roamed and could move on his own recognizance. Later I was surprised to hear the term "Monster." It was old to us by the time it became a household word.

I like the four- and five-man rush against the good passing team. I don't believe linebackers can continually matchup against the excellence of the quick-footed receivers today. I still believe a passing attack, like I said earlier, can backfire if you put enough of a rush and get enough hands of defensive linemen in the thrower's lane. The structure of the pass defense lies in the ability to penetrate and harass the passer.

Over the last decade we have averaged about 3.4 sacks per game. We find that reflects an excellent ratio for getting pass rush into the enemy backfield. The defenders today must be specialists themselves. We tell our pass rushers, "Everything they legislate is aimed at keeping you off the quarterback's body. It is a great challenge today to be a pass-rusher. You have to be tremendous athletes in excellent shape. You need the start, the agility and the competitive spirit as never before."

You can't make a man faster, but we continue to drill on getting off the mark and putting on heavy pressure and containing the quarterback. I will not tolerate a secondary blaming the pass rush or the pass rush blaming the secondary. The passing percentages go up yearly. It has to be a delicate balance of cooperation between rusher and defender to show the passing game's efficiency. But like I pointed out earlier, the passing game can quickly self-destruct and ruin its own attack momentum. It is still a play that requires artful execution between two men with a moving object. There are so many variables if you figure in weather, turf, condition of the ball and the vision of the thrower. A passing team actually possesses many more opportunities for defenses to make a vital play than going against the running control teams.

When it comes to sides and agility on defense, I tell our men that a 200-pounder at the right position and angle can take down any pro runner in the game. I have played and won titles with 170 pound nose-guards. I have had 168-pound defensive ends. I have had 175-pound linebackers. You can't give away 45-pounds-a-man all day but a defense is only as good as its reaction. The pursuit of three agile 190-pounders to the point of impact can be as effective as one burly 270-pounder.

I love to watch Alabama's gang tackling smaller teams of 20 years ago. They pursued like barracudas after the kill. I insist that we get to the ball. Again concentration. Selling. We must get to the ball with as many numbers as possible because that is the St. John's way. Something else: because we spend so much more time on polishing drills and timing than scrimmaging, like heavy-duty drills teams do, we like to think we make fewer defensive mistakes as far as off-sides and encroachments are concerned. I tell my men that penalties come only when you are not concentrating; only when you are thinking about something other than the snap of the ball.

I have mentioned that defenses have personalities as distinct as people. Many times that is based on size or mobility. If a team is smaller, it must bide its time, give up the smaller chunks of ground and hope to make the big play. A larger, active team can challenge the offense on the line of scrimmage. We like to use little stunts and we will blitz only when we believe it will disrupt certain teams whose quarterbacks might not pick it up as quickly as others! We blitz perhaps once every 9.5 plays. But we like to move our men around, throw off the blocking angles and have as much fun on defense as we do on offense.

I urge young coaches in high schools, particularly, not to be afraid to innovate on defense. In my high school days there were times I'd set up a nine-man front, then come up a gap on one side and a five-man line and then throw a three-man line with six linebackers. Any high school underdog should come equipped with a dozen varieties of radical defensive changes. I tell my men, "If something's going wrong and you can't seem to top them, try anything—jump into a seven-man line or shoot two linebackers. Never let the offense run something so consistently it feels it owns you.

I used to love to watch George Allen's defenses. He made the offense think and maybe forced more audibles than any coach in the country.

I have never been able to understand how a team will stay in the same defensive alignments when they are getting eaten up. That is nonsense. You are asking to be butchered and quartered.

When the other team is building momentum, particularly if you are behind, you must force a turnover—or make a rousing play. This is best done by putting on all-out blitzes or showing radically different fronts or letting the linebackers roam free. If penetration doesn't work, let everybody in sight dive into a mass on the line of scrimmage. Never give a rolling tank a downhill grade without a booby trap.

Oh yes, the so-called nickel and dime defenses and the prevent defense: I don't buy it in college—or the pros for that matter. I ask you a simple question: why give the offense, which may have been stumbling, the chance to get back into the game?

The coach who says he wants a dime defense and puts in all his defensive backs, in reality, is saying, "I don't trust my defensive line to harass the passer."

I have seen teams again and again regain momentum and turn the game around by finally initialing a destructive passing game after having trouble with four- and five-man lines and solid threes all afternoon. Give the good passer time and he will find that target for 55 percent completions. Check out the percent defense and you will find as I have that many times a 40-percent passer suddenly becomes a 70-percent passer imbued with the confidence of jungle monarchs.

I always remember what Fred Shero, a magnificent hockey coach, said: "The game plan that's good enough to bring you the lead is good enough to hold it."

How true. That's why I will never forget a defensive alignment that has held the team in check for 50 minutes and switch suddenly to what I call the "panic array." Oh, I may caution my safety men to play a shade deeper and under no circumstances let the receiver get behind them. And I may tell my linemen to call on all their agility and charge to get to the passer—but aside from this, a defense that has contained for most of the afternoon should be relied on to sustain the lead down the stretch.

I have even had players ask why we don't use the prevent defense of the pros. I tell them that our defensive plan was calculated to win over the 60-minute mark. I see no reason why we should suddenly become so sensitive and worried over a foe we have been handling nicely.

I urge you to try new things on defense. I urge you to look at the versatility of your players. Perhaps that little 150-pound kid with the dirty nose and solid under-pinnings can make it in high school at middle guard. I know one fine prep team that averaged just 166 pounds on defense up front. It made jokes of the 220-pound blockers.

But as I said, in college it gets tougher because the big men are good men. Still, there is a place in high schools and smaller colleges today for gutsy, tough, feisty little men up front. I have never disqualified a lineman because of his size. I've always said if he thinks he can handle bigger men, I will never discourge him.

A wise man once said, "It is for want of application rather than shortage of gifts, that men fail in their search for success."

On football defense, that is so true. I have seen large, maneuverable defenses fall prey for lack of coordination, leadership and willingness to change philosophy. In contrast to staying with an attack which is doing the job, I have seen so many losing defenses stay vulnerable rather than try something new.

That can be the fault of a coach who believes his initial plan is the only one. That can be the fault of players who don't accept change. That can be the fault of physical ailings which preclude the shifting of men.

But I believe most defenses can improve if given the confidence; if, once having decided on the personality and traits of that defense, the coach inspires it. Defense is an emotional thing. All the large bodies on the earth can't function at peak performance if they aren't motivated. They can't sustain power without character and a cohesiveness of ambition and desire. That wills victories.

The coach who says, "We've lost everything on defense. We'll be small and inexperienced and vulnerable," is doing his squad a gross injustice. There are all sizes and shapes on that team, which will play fanatically for a just cause."

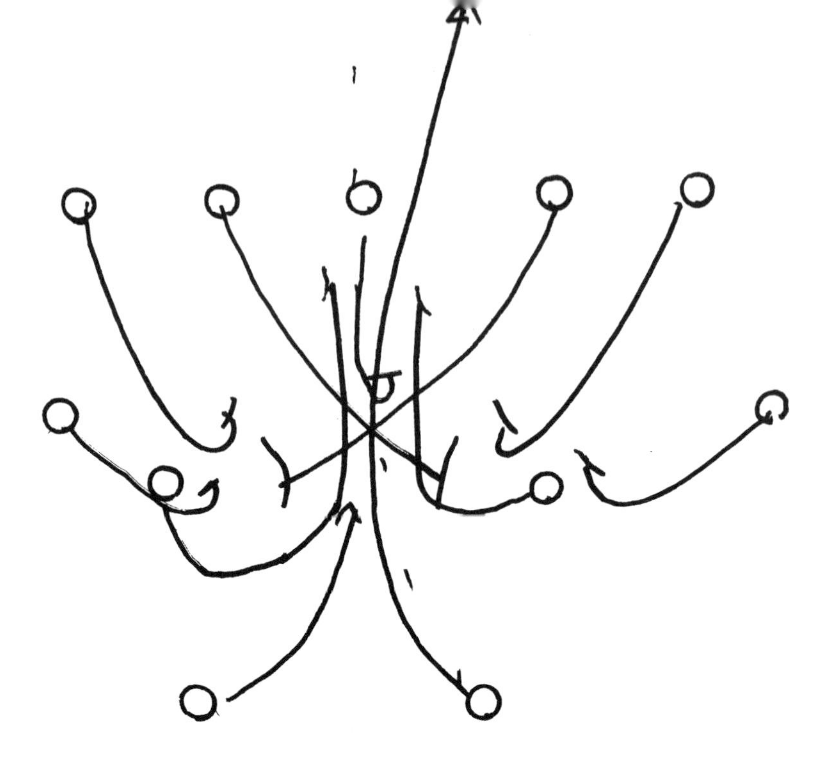

Putting the Kick in the Kickoff Return

Long before it was fashionable, we worked hard at our kickoff returns. They have always been a specialty with us and I think that is why we led our conference seven times with them.

Kickoff-return men are a special breed. I remember St. Thomas College's Popcorn Brandt saying while he played with the Pittsburgh Steelers, "I say a quick prayer and then head up the middle. It's like going into a dark tunnel and knowing you're going to hit a freight train head on."

We've had some remarkable return carriers like Jim Lehmann, Casey Vilandre, Tom White, Jerry Haugen and Joe Luby. Some were truly great, using blockers and instinct hand-in-hand. In other places and other times, they might have been point-men on caravans, Kamikaze pilots, stuntmen or warrior leaders.

They must be truly swift and fearless.

Our two deep men field the ball and the one who does not carry the ball moves up to block as do the fullback and ends. Our guards try to kick out the first two men down the field. All the others simply try to ride their men out of the area.

A great runner like Haugen will smell out the hole and many times it will open other than the area in which we set up the blocking. Nothing is predictable in kickoff returns. Opponents many times over-react to what we are trying to do and it plays into our runner's hands. In this case a crack will open in unexpected terrain and our runner will roar up field if he is alert.

The kickoff return is not difficult but it requires concentrated practice so that everyone knows where he is supposed to be. The unsung heroes, of course, are the linemen who find the soft underbellies of the enemy coverage and slash it open, enabling the darting backs to make the long gains.

We've had 99-yard returns and nine-yard returns. I worry only about one thing on kickoffs: Fumbles.

On on-side kickoffs I stress to the linemen that they should never try to be a hero; just get onto the ball and hold on.

The kickoff return, like the punt, is a weapon of devastating proportions to the morale of both teams. It can sap a defense's morale. It can hype your own. It is a play that should be worked on often—with nothing left up to chance. Extemporaneous offshoots will develop that are not planned for. But basically getting the blockers into position and the runner knowing which path he must start on, are the vital igredients.

11
Anatomy of an Important Victory

Call it a turning point or rave about the ivy-colored tradition. Every team has a turning point in its schedule. It may be a new power arising. It may be the old power entrenched. It may be the game for the league title. It may be the game the alumni want to win above all others. Usually "the game" is a battle which is remembered by both teams for its uplifting or devastating effect on a year.

One of our natural foes is the always formidable College of St. Thomas team in St. Paul. For years we have battled the Toms in the so-called naturals where blue chips were stacked high and where crowds were noisy and enthusiastic. Our battles usually are preceded by the tail-gating outings where thousands of alumni return for afternoon or early evening partying in the parking lots. By the time the chiding and joshing and reminiscing is over and the kickoff is approaching, the intensity of the rivalry can be felt from the bottom row to the top.

A new, energetic and imaginative St. Thomas coach, Mark Deinhart, has capitalized on the natural traditions of our rivalry to help make this more than just a game. It has become an event. A local writer has tabbed him "Marvelous Mark" engaging in shootouts with "Black Gag," or yours truly.

It's fun. The young fireballing coach with innovations and a wide-open hell-for-leather style against the establishment—if I may call our St. John's football program that.

Two recent games have been classics. The thousands who witnessed them have given our performances an A for effort and entertainment. The ball has moved, the games have been close, the elements of surprise, key performance and courage have all been involved. It is a pleasure to gear up for St. Thomas with its dynamic passing game, and I'd like to share with you a typical week of preparation for THE games:

The mental preparation actually started during the dinner after the previous Saturday's victory. We didn't take enough time to uncoil and relax, I'll admit. Right after the victory, a reporter asked, "How about St. Thomas? Are you thinking about them?" I answered, "Hey, give us time to enjoy this one. St Thomas will be on our minds enough."

I didn't tell him the seeds of the St. Thomas game were planted in my mind unconsciously the moment the last game had ended. Walking to the dressing room I was thinking, "How much better will we have to be next week?"

Unlike Scarlett O'Hara in "Gone With The Wind," I have trouble setting aside concern. I can't seem to equate with her pet theory, "I'll worry about that tomorrow." I begin the worrying process for the big ones almost immediately.

But I managed to take my wife out and for a few hours tried to lose track of the preparation and intensity we faced ahead. I urge every coach to try and enjoy the fruits of victory immediately before embarking on another course of concern. I fight it. I try. That night I managed to have a dance or two with Peggy, but driving home I was saying, "Why can't this last? Why can't a coach get more time to savor the fruits?"

Sharing:

"The athlete who learns to share in football will also learn to share in his work ethic and in his marriage. Sharing in his life is everything."

Sunday morning: It's video time, time to study the tapes of the previous day's game. Are we executing right? Are we blocking the right people? I go over each position, each man's job. On every snap every man has an assignment. Not until you study the films are you sure who has executed to the fullest and who has missed on what plays. I study the moves, the reactions, the precision of execution. I make notes. I keep asking the one prime question: did the man miss his assignment because of bad coaching—or is he unable to execute it physically? This is the time for soul-searching, when the game is fresh in your mind. If it is a coaching problem, I must act quickly to straighten out any questions the player has. If it is one of execution and physical, I must look for a new man to replace him.

We don't grade the players. I just make perhaps half a dozen mental calculations and a few more notes on mistakes I want to see corrected quickly. You don't need grading to tell if the cogs are fitting into the over 11 machines.

Note this, we do not hold Sunday meetings as so many teams do. We feel this is a day of rest. Mental and physical. It's like a pitstop in a race: time to plot strategy, refill the tank, bite the bullet and get refreshed. Never do I have a player look at the films for an hour or so. I tell them, "Forget it now and we'll think about it Monday. Enjoy yesterday's game."

Monday: And it's time to let the team look at the real films. I pointed out a few easily identifiable problems. For instance, our foe scored on a long pass. I mentioned that St. Thomas will know this and has an excellent passing team. We must expect that they will try to hit us on the same play. Also, last week's rivals had success rolling out and our ends were not containing them. I told them we must concentrate on the long pass and the roll-outs because St. Thomas was adept at both. I told the squad that beyond that I thought they played a fine game and should feel proud.

While we hold no practice on Mondays, we do have a team meeting. We held a film session at 4 p.m. When I was a younger coach I used to practice and watch films. I find that's too long for a Monday session. There is another day to charge the physical plant and build up the adrenalin.

We had decided after the films that we needed better passing routes for our receivers. I told them that St. Thomas was so big that we had to go around or over them. In most years we had played St. Thomas the last game of the year—many times in blizzards or on wind-blown frozen turf. I told them it made no difference when we played at St. Thomas since this early season game had to give us good weather. I felt the squad was relaxed and ready for a week of solid concentration. I was beginning to feel my own adrenalin flow. I thought, "This is what makes the world go around. This is what coaching's all about. The big game."

If you can't get up for the old rivals, if you don't get that sense of urgency and even a little quiet desperation, get out of the game.

For a time I had considered showing last year's St. Thomas game—a thriller we had won 24-23, but I decided against it. I didn't want to give them too much to think about. But as I walked home I had some misgivings. I decided that, too, was natural. When a coach doesn't second-guess himself, he's certainly in no position to second-guess the players.

We still had four days to get ready for the Tommies. I was sure that's all we'd need.

The next move Monday was to meet with the coaches and figure up the plusses and minuses of the previous game. We went over the key plays and decided we had made progress where we needed it. Then we turned our attention toward the Tommies. Our scouting reports were of little use. The Tommies had waylaid a weak foe in the opener. We could gain nothing from evaluating that game, so we turned to films of last year's Tommy edition — which had used virtually the same integral players to provide us with that one-point heart- stopper.

We asked ourselves how many defensive adjustments we'd have to make for their fast-hitting offensive style. We knew their veteran quarterback, Randy Muezel, was confident and tough and could run or pass and knew all the tricks for keeping a defense off balance.

Versatility:
"Why shouldn't players be able to switch positions? It's only a game—and they are all athletes or they wouldn't be playing."

We studied the films and again became acutely aware of all the Tommies' movements. They are like trying to handle a sack of snakes. They do so much shifting, show so much man-in-motion that we knew they would give us more we hadn't even seen. We also knew their quarterback was a competent scrambler who, if he got out of pocket, could run us into the ground. We decided we could slow down their running game but that we must use haste and thoroughness at the same time to shore up our passing defense.

So our primary work would be aimed at getting a rush on the Tommy passer.

Notice: we try to simplify our objective down to one or two or three basic fundamentals to concentrate on. Never try to expose a team to so many goals or so many innovations that they lose track of the prime fact: they are a good football team to begin with and have nothing to fear, but a few little additions and a little more concentration in certain areas is prime insurance.

Now we looked at their defense and studied what our offenses must do to be effective. We knew their defense liked to stunt, to surprise you with varied fronts and to try to take your attention off your primary objectives. I pondered if they used approximately the same defense they did a year ago. Would they use the monster defense? Would they play the four deep?

It now becomes a guessing game, a real war of nerves. I could feel my skin tingle. This must be how history's great generals felt as they prepared their last-minute battle plans. It has to make you tighten up a bit and dry your throat. This is the St. Thomas team that can ruin your game with defensive breakthroughs and they can break down a team's offensive morale by their blitzing and sacking.

We tried to think of all the possibilities of all the devious moves and the subtle twists their bright young coach could be conjuring up. I tried to think as Mark would think. I thought: "How would I try to stop St. John's." It was a magnificent guessing game. In reality, the battle would be decided in the pits in the ability of the players to execute their basics. But for now, the "generals" in the war rooms were having a delightful time.

Our coaching staff diagramed the dozens of stunts and blitzing styles of defense the Tommies could use. We knew we must be careful and precise in our blocking because their defensive quickness could raise havoc. We also knew we'd have to give them an edge in size. Speed-wise I believed we were comparable.

That evening walking home I concentrated on three of our offensivemen: quarterback Denny Schleper, running back Rick Bell and jack-of-all-trades Chuck Williams.

Williams came to us a 135-pound, asthma-plagued youngster of the rankest walk-on caliber. But his intelligence, additional 30 pounds and penchant for turning on his speed at the right times, plus his combativeness, signaled me that he was something special to our team, perhaps the difference between being merely a contender and a champion. I decided Williams might be the element to tip the balance.

Also, we had another small, first-year starter in Pat Pederson we thought they might underestimate. I thought more and more about Williams and Pederson Monday evening. I knew they would have heavy coverage on Bell; either running he'd be keyed or pass receiving he'd be double-teamed.

I have learned long ago we must have more than one man. But the surprise man can't be ushered into places where his morale can be broken. But I felt emotionally and temperamentally that Williams and Pederson were ready. Williams, particularly, could be valuable if he could hold up both ways, for he was one of our most reliable defensive backs as well as returning kickoffs and punts.

Tuesday: And it's a day of methodical preparation. Little talk about the Tommies in particular. Now we're building our resources. We had eight by 10 inch flash cards with St. Thomas formations and defense on them. Our scout team simulates the St. Thomas plays. On the cards we used red ink to emphasize the Tommy plays we considered their bread and butter operations. I decided we'd use two primary defenses—a five-man line and pro three with heavy coverage in the secondary.

Now that's radical for us! Also, we put in a few more stunts. We continued to emphasize the pass rush and containing the quarterback.

The drills ran smoothly. Only a few questions. I felt the team was well in control of itself. I also had a sneaking suspicion that St. Thomas, despite throwing 50 passes in its first game, would try to out-muscle us and make use of its husky line. I pointed out that we could expect a war up front and that we must get off the mark. No sloppy tackling. We must let their bigger men know they can't intimidate us. I repeated how I felt about their passing if an aerial blitz came. "We'll turn it against them. A couple of interceptions, a couple of sacks and a few bad throws and it will be going our way."

I felt confident. But I felt, also, that we might need a break to win. Again I am proud of the St. John's way... the poise we have shown through the years. I said to myself, "We have beaten St. Thomas far more than it has beaten us in my coaching career. They are the ones that must be asking 'When will we blow it? When will St. John's get unlucky? We expect to win. They have to wonder if they CAN win."

Wednesday: I decided to put in the offensive wrinkles for Williams. We'll try some different things. Lone passes to him. Wide reverses perhaps. We must work him into the offense more than just as a special teams man. His speed, I felt, could be the difference. I also knew we needed to shore up kick coverage teams. Needed a couple of head-hunters. One fellow was a splendid centerfielder in baseball and I concluded he must be a good athlete. I inserted him on our coverage team and he looked mobile and agressive in drills.

The long pass plays to Williams looked good—as did his wide and inside reverses. He seemed to be able to play any position. I had to smile to myself: If the Toms go for a handful of Bell, they may get a throatful of Williams.

Thursday: And Williams' plays were installed. If the Toms concentrate on our bootleg, he will score on a reverse, I was certain. I find Williams loves to go deep. I told Schleper to call a deep pass to Williams any time he thinks the defense is tightening up. I told my wife that I've found new dimension. I could feel the team getting excited about the way our little Williams and Pederson were working. Either could be a star Saturday.

Age:
"Who says getting old is becoming comfortable. In coaching it's a thorn."

But a steady rain settled in late Thursday and into Friday. The field becomes a quagmire. I wondered if our impetus would be denied. I wondered if we would be peaking. Intrusions piled up. I was accused by some of the media of pouring it on in our opener when we tried a field goal with a lead as time ran out and I pleaded, "temporary insanity."

I found time in the locker room to tell the team, "Remember, to us this is another game. To St. Thomas it is the seventh game of a World Series. Nothing is going to stop us. We'll find a way to win and St. Thomas will find a way to lose. That's been the history the last 25 years. And you are a good team—one that can be a great team. Forget the rain and the field. St. John's knows how to beat St. Thomas."

Friday: Made it a short day. The difficulty of that day was cutting the 105-man squad to the traveling limit of 48. I hate this job. It's the worst thing about the profession. The glazed stares from the borderline players, the look of hurt from the young fellows who think they're moving up.

This is a 90-mile trip and we planned the bus ride almost to the split second. We want to eat our meal for the 7:30 p.m. game four hours before kickoff. We eat at 2:45 and leave on the bus at 3:45 p.m. Never do I want to arrive too early. I sensed at Friday practice the team is loose but thinking football.

We do something at St. John's that few teams do. We let the players who live in the Twin Cities go home the night before a game in that area. The 45-minute loosening-up drills went smoothly. The team appeared to be peaking. But who knows until the first hit?

So we went over the next day's activities, jokingly told the players who would stay in their Twin Cities homes to try to make it before the second half, urged the players to put out their best effort, which I told them would be good enough to win. And I reminded them that St. Thomas-St. John's games are the ones they'll probably always remember most, the kind that form indelible pictures on the memory.

I also pointed out that this is one fine St. Thomas team — perhaps its best in many years. But it is meeting a fine St. John's team and that we have lost to the Toms only twice in some 25 meetings. I told them we still have the mystique and the intangibles going for us, plus, I think, fine preparation.

Saturday: And it's D-day. I told the squad in a brief speech before the game that "This is the day we've waited for. It won't all go smoothly but I have confidence we will, like St. John's teams always seem to do, find a way. Remember: expect the good things to happen. They'll be waiting for the bad ones to happen. Keep coming back no matter what. That's the mark of a champion—the teams that can get off the floor."

The game was a classic; poetry of motion, movement and suspense. I was enthralled myself. I had mentioned so often during the week that our primary aim was a minimum of mistakes, that if mistakes were made it would be the Tommies who make them. But Deinhart's team was beautifully prepared. The match-up of styles and techniques was exquisite. This is what makes football so noble; two fine teams matched in a probing, prodding way until lightning lights up the sky and field.

But mistakes came. A bad snap over the St. Thomas punter's head. I hoped St. Thomas believed it was snake-bitten. Eventually we surged to the lead—but had to repel a desperate, well-conceived St. Thomas comeback in the last one minute and 47 seconds that used 14 plays to march 70 yards in a magnificent piece of execution and control. In this span we made two pass interferences. The Toms completed six more. But time ran out and we won another thriller 27-21.

All of the men performed well. But Williams was a standout. At 170 pounds he played both ways. He intercepted two passes, made seven solo tackles and four assists. On offense he was the man who turned the tide, as we thought he might. He was a continuous thorn in the Tommy defense. He caught seven passes for

169 yards, rushed for 57, including 22 on that special reverse. Pederson contributed with several slashing driving runs. This took the pressure off Bell, who made another big contribution. Schleper's passing was brilliant throughout.

Our team was jubilant and I felt that we might have turned the corner. Our dimensions suddenly were 30 percent greater than before the game. We had won the St. John's way by outlasting a time-honored foe.

I felt so good that I wanted it to last forever. In fact, it wasn't until Peggy asked around 11 p.m., "Who do we get next?" that I began to worry once more. But it was a nice, warm worry.

12
The St. John's Blocking System

Critics do a double-take when I tell them we have used the same St. John's blocking system for 30 years through hundreds of rule changes and modifications. We emphasize and insist on blocking low and staying low and keeping on your feet. Sometimes we use the chop block. Again the constant stress of repetitions and drills and timing and finesse. I can pull out a 1953 film and you will see the same kind of St. John's blocking, hopefully low and sharp and precise.

Basically, we believe in sustaining the block, keeping with the defensive man. Our differences, however, in several things stand out in comparison to others.

Most teams block ends on contact. With us, the block starts when we make contact. The leg power, the concentration and the snap. I like to think St. John's blockers stay with their men just a split second longer. One arm in tight, free arm giving leverage and drive. And I have stressed so much the problem of holding penalties. Heads up—to give solid blocking surface.

Of course, we don't block against dummies. I have always told the team, you're not blocking dummies in a game so why practice against them. The dummy is immobile. Why develop blocking angles on a machine when in the game the opponent is moving, thinking, changing techniques and angles.

"Sustain that block!" is an order you'll hear cracking across the St. John's practice field. "Stay with the man!"...it is imperative that the blocker stay in contact with the defender as long as possible. Just imagine the importance. If the two or three key blockers on every play can blow their men just that extra two-tenths of a second, that gives the attacking back perhaps six or seven steps. In that time he can gain another five yards, change directions, cut against the grain, break into the open or pick up enough speed to gain the momentum to carry the eventual tackler another three yards.

I'll tell you how important blocking is. Let's say on 40 running plays you add two-tenths of a second to the block—stay with the man that much longer. That could reflect as much as 125 more running yards. Or seven or eight more first downs. What coach wouldn't trade his car for such consistently better statistics. It all comes with the block.

Blocking is so much more mental preparation than physical that I never worry about the initial hitting contact during the game. If my players have run off 200 plays and angled in on 200 blocking assignments in our precision and timing drills, they'll have the mental equipment ready to go on Saturday; they will be again like hungry animals coming out of the cages searching for food.

A player just this season told me, "John, when I got here I was really worried about not throwing a real block against real people or real equipment. I thought I'd be gun shy. But in the First Game everything I worked on was transferred right to the game. I was amazed. I could hardly wait for contact."

Surprised? Don't be. The charging up period of no-contact drills, I believe, is a vital emotion and psychological part of the game — heavy ammunition for the Saturday clash.

A philosopher once observed, "If we are to live like brutes and survive, we must count on experience well reasoned out." We do just that. For that hour on Saturday we may be reasonably compared to brutes. I count on the experience of 35 years of coaching—and we certainly try to reason out all week what will work when the time to be "brutes" appears.

Let's dig a bit deeper into this philosophy of preparing to block real people in a meaningful situation after only thinking about it all week.

Let's go back to boxing, which is easily equated with our team. You don't see a champion or challenger fighting all out in 10 or 15 round duels every day. No, the ones I have seen work on speed, the light bag, running, balance and then, for perhaps four or five rounds, still don't unleash their weapons or engage in all-out combative competition. No, one fighter will work on his jab. Another will work on sliding punches. Another will work on his foot speed and mobility. Another will work on in-fighting.

You could well ask Sugar Ray Leonard, "How can you be ready at fight time if you haven't been catching punches all week? How can you be ready to unleash your awesome combination when you have't tried them for real all week or maybe even since the last fight?" I'm sure Sugar Ray would tell you, as he told a newspaper friend of mine before the Tommy Hearns fight, "I will win with speed—not slugging. So I'm working on speed."

And, speed, of course, was the eventual difference. Speed and timing. But Sugar Ray knew he didn't have to engage in all-out bloody ring wars every day. He geared himself mentally. He approached the fight with the proper discipline.

We try the same things in the St. John's way; we know what we want to do and we work on our minds, imprinting the type and kind of blocks we want to throw. Then we execute them continually. We don't have to knock down people to know they will work. We believe they will and our precision and timing is honed to a degree that the block is automatic. Whether there is a live body in front or not is purely academic.

Let me make another point about blocking during drills—I mean the actual knock-down, drag-out kind: Early in my career I tried a blocking practice drill called "Bull in the Ring." I believe many schools still use it. You place a man — supposedly a defensive man—in the middle of a circle of blockers, each of whom has a number. The defensive man has no idea who the numbers are. You call a number and a blocker leaps out of the ring and charges in to block the man in the middle. He has no idea where the blocker is coming from but must show alertness to fend off the blocker to the best of his ability. It supposedly teaches ingenuity, agility and gives the blocker some muscle to gun for.

Instead, in our camp a fine young player, Dick Miller, had two ribs cracked when he got blind-sided. I said, that's the end. What possible good can come from an exercise the likes of which would ever or rarely crop up in a game. Using the "Bull in the Ring" or something similar might be fine in the commandos, but we're preparing for a football game — not a midnight commando raid.

English scholar Frederick Robertson said that faith creates power, that doubt cramps energy. We continue to impress on our team that it has every reason for faith in the no-contact blocking drills because we win with them. I have never heard a St. John's player complain after a loss that we were whipped because "we didn't hit people in the practices." No, if we are beaten, it is by the other teams executing exceptionally well and we having provided them with opportunities by mistakes.

I've had smaller men tell me, in fact, that they believed their careers were preserved by the very fact we were not risking injuries during the week. One 150-pounder said, "I'm good for a dozen big blocks during the game, John, but I wouldn't want to be doing it all week."

Because of our constant play drills, I believe our downfield blocking has been just a bit better than our foes over the years. I mean that we are working on starts, balance, movement. They are far more important than collisions. Getting to the point of impact at the correct time and angle is everything. I know that some offensive linemen hate their work. Here we try to make it fun. We tell them it isn't a game of raw strength, that they don't have to be plow horses or blacksmiths. We tell them that they are thinkers, which they are; they are out to out-guess out-maneuver, out-angle the rival. We try to make it fun. Like I said, Saturday can be the day of the brute and the beast. But let's go in unhampered by injuries, our assignments clear in our heads and our bodies fresh enough to explode in maximum movement for the 60 minutes. I think you do that better by saving the contact for the showdown.

Again, as in tackling, I have that brief moment of fear—will the blockers be able to stand the first blows of bone on bone? In one game, I had three blockers shaken up in the first five minutes. I asked myself,"Is this the end?" No, it was a freak series of plays. We didn't have a dizzy head the rest of the day and won going away.

Let's talk about baseball for a moment, since all sports are inter-related and work on the mental aspects as well as the physical. How often have you seen a major league club scrimmage itself for nine innings on the off-day? Never. But each man may go into his little acre and work on hitting curve balls or shagging flies.

In tennis, I notice competitors smashing the ball relentlessly against a wall, working on speed, footwork and handling various caroms. To improve you must concentrate on your own skills in your own way. Bashing heads or engaging in heavy contact skirmishes in practices often may only encourage bad habits. You don't have the time or quality of teaching or observation to make little corrections in your own games if your are worried about jolting someone or making or missing a point.

Practice, remember fellow coaches, is just that; a time to perfect your own abilities—not to limit them or risk them by incurring injuries or creating doubts.

"The St. John's block," I once heard a young coach try to explain at a clinic, "is really made in the head—during the huddle." I loved that. I commended the young man. He said, " For years I've seen St. John's play and marveled at the players' ability to make the right block at the vital time. Then I watched your practices. I know what you mean when you say, 'Believe in the system.' I believe and I am trying to get others to think like that." Of course, the day everybody is sold on "blocking of the mind," I may be through. I don't think I could handle nine foes playing the "St. John's way."

I once heard a coach stress heavy power blocking and double-teaming with "superior force" and he explained that he "scrimmaged his men with ferocity twice a week because only the survivors would play well on Saturday." That was early in the year. He lost four of the last five and I heard him explain, "Injuries wiped us out."

Faith:

"I ask only one thing of my teams: have faith in themselves."

I was curious. I set out to make a check of newspapers and magazines and anyplace I could find where the injury story could be reliably understood. Out of 100 major college teams I checked, 42 blamed losing seasons on injuries. As close as I could come to an estimate, over 3,000 man-games were lost by starters through injuries to these 100 teams. One team had 11 out of 22 regulars miss from two to seven games. Exactly 55 percent of these injuries were suffered in practice! Overall, the figure was close to 40 percent in practices for these teams.

That is shocking. It tells us, however, a candid story of what is wrong with battering practices in drills—if we listen and learn.

Hockey teams are notorious for getting people hurt in scrimmages. I compare that with Indianapolis 500-mile auto racers. You don't see six or seven of these murderously fast cars racing each other at Indianapolis six or seven times to get used to the Memorial holiday classic. Why? Because they are working on their own particular gifts and skills and special equipment, honing it like we do at St. John's.

Does it make any sense to crack up a specially-prepared classic racing machine because the crew wanted to "get the feel" of the race beforehand? That would be nonsense.

St. John's blocking, thusly, combines the belief that it will work with constant execution in signal drill against the defensive teams merely holding the position while the blockers merely rush to their men and feign the block. If he thinks it is a bad angle or suggests we take the defensive man another direction, splendid. We talk it over and try out new suggestions. We try to make it a game of chess—of skills; not flying bodies.

I go back to the chapter on contact where I point out that, if there is weakness in our preparation, it is that we don't see enough honest knock-down hammering to know which men have more heart than others. But in watching films, that is quickly discernible.

Oh sometimes, like all coaches, I am guilty of not shuffling personnel quickly enough while questioning a man's ability to absorb contact punishment. But by his junior year, I know who goes above and beyond the line of duty, who is not that serious about the game and who would rather be strolling in the park with the pretty brunette.

One season I benched a man for lack of solid blocking the last three games—but he came back in tigerish fashion the next year. Another time, I recall clearly being guilty of staying with a junior too long when a sophomore would give his life to knock down a brick wall for St. John's. But ordinarily, if you study the films closely, the lack of contact by a man is clearly evidenced. I then generally ask, "Is there something you'd rather be doing than knocking people down in the game?" He usually gets the message.

In all my years of coaching, I've only had seven or eight players I can remember who couldn't improve their hitting skills in the games. One told me honestly, "I love the drills but I can't bring myself to get jarred up in the real thing." I asked if he came to St. John's because he heard the practices were light. "Yes," he explained, "but somebody steered me wrong about the games. I thought they'd be touch football."

I had an assistant who left because he had no faith in the system. Years later he called to say he was a head coach and was using most of our ideas.

I'm glad I never have to play him.

TWO OF HIS ALL-TIME FAVORITES, star pass-catching end Mike Grant and his famous father, Bud, who recently retired as the Minnesota Vikings coach, chat with Gag.

13
Selling Your School

An Eastern paper once said the beautiful thing about St. John's was that we didn't set out to sell the school. The recruits and students sold themselves.

I have heard coaches complain about the ethics of their schools; about the administrative process; about their school's rigidity; about their school's "lack of understanding of the value of sports." Goodness. If every college or high school could equate with what the coach envisioned as the perfect institution, no staff would ever change, no new faces would ever appear and no progress would be made. Progress comes from agitation, the mixing and melting of different ideas.

Lord. Wouldn't it be nice for John Gagliardi if St. John's would give him a dozen scholarships and build at least another 2,500 stands and try to develop one of those glistening marching bands. At least import 20 pompom girls from nearby St. Benedict's. I mean, what would it hurt if we at least enlarged and glamorized the union a bit? My office certainly could use a secretary and a library.

The coach first must ask himself if his program is in the proper perspective; if, shall we say, the whole athletic program is counting on it for support. Then he's in a high-powered situation where he'd better demand everything he can get because the day he loses, the whole department will be up in arms.

I could certainly make a point for flying to games or being quartered in the best hotels. Or how about the car dealer loaning me a few new sports cars just to park around and impress the recruits?

Fortunately, I find St. John's football at just the niche it deserves; a healthy program with boys playing for fun, pretty St. Benedict's girls to make it interesting, loud but not profane rooters and a score of intellectual honesty about the whole situation. Maybe the Benedictine monks are the answer. For everyone who enjoys the game there are two that would prefer to write, read, study or attend devotions during our contests.

There are no campus parades when we won national championships. I think somebody did buy me lunch in the student cafeteria. I got lots of nice letters. I was asked to speak six or seven times around the vicinity. But in two weeks, everyone was back studying the really important things in life. Football at St. John's, you see, is a diversion—not a staple.

Making a college choice is a major event in a young person's life. Hey, this is four years out of your life. You are transported to a new location, new friends, new atmosphere.

I recall two brothers I was hoping to land. One took a look at our beautiful but sometimes quiet campus and said, "Hey, this is for me. I need time and some quiet to study. I just like the looks of the place—you know the trees and lakes and some of the old buildings."

His brother looked at him like he was crazy: "This is the kind of place you go stir crazy. Give me the bright lights."

Both became standout athletes. Both made the right choices. Both are successes in life. Never try to sell a boy that your school has everything. Just try to sell him that it may have the things that he'll enjoy best and supply him with the set of values he's looking for.

There was a newspaper article praising our program that pointed out that we seemed to know how to balance the benefits of sports and studies. I would have to say that I never coached a boy at St. John's who didn't first want to come here to study. Football was secondary. We try to let the school sell itself. If I happen to be taking a prospect across the campus, I will call over two or three other students and just ask simply: "Do you like it here?" Ninety-nine percent are enthusiastic. I've been lucky.

I recall strolling through the campus with Mike Grant, a fine prospect and son of the Minnesota Viking coach. The first three youngsters I brought over all were ecstatic about the place. Bud called me aside and suggested, "Why not quit while you're ahead?"

Of course, Mike came here and was an all-around favorite with the students and team. He's coaching high school now and I say that he epitomized the St. John's program so well I'd love to see him return here someday as a coach.

When I talk to recruits I try to study the boy. I watch his reactions as we stroll around the campus. If he inquires quickly about the "fun places" or the "good restaurants," I have to tell him that perhaps he isn't St. John's material. The boy who is interested in St. John's values usually isn't that much concerned where the watering spas are located or why there isn't more neon.

But I have been fooled.

One young man epitomized big-city swagger from the top of his $20 haircut to his tailored jeans. He seemed completely out of place, I thought, as he asked how many touring road companies brought good shows to the area. He almost seemed to ignore the scenery or the accounts of school life put to him by students. He talked little about the sports program and seemed almost bored when I brought up academics.

I was the most surprised man on campus when the youngster showed up and became an all-conference performer and an excellent track man. I asked him about his decision one time and he replied, "Almost overnight I came to realize that the things I really wanted weren't the flash and the nightlife. After a year of St. John's I knew that I really wanted close friends, good instructors and a sense of a strong school tie."

WINNING QUARTERBACK JOHN GAGLIARDI, JR. with sister and brother offering congratulations.

Since that time, I learned never to prejudge the recruits.

Another told me, "I guess this isn't for me, Mr. Gagliardi, It's just a little too woodsy—know what I mean?" I laughed and agreed he didn't resemble a lumberjack in the least.

But he transferred in two years later and gave us a brilliant senior year of football and was one of the most popular men on the campus. He explained, "Hey, this place is for somebody who is a little more mature than I was as a freshman. Your values change, you know."

Indeed. I am not saying that St. John's or the small college in the rural areas are the best for all mature, deep-thinking young men. That is ridiculous. But a city youngster has to experience this way of life before he can adequately judge, I believe.

It reminds me of a young man who transferred from here for a semester to a large, bustling campus. He returned quickly and explained, "It was so cold and fast-moving I used to give the Moonies on campus a buck just to have somebody to talk to." He explained the things he missed most were the intimacy, the contact and the conversations which develop so readily on a smaller campus.

You've heard of big university football players who never have a thing in common once they leave the practice field—outside of sharing a squad dinner. Not here. We have consistently developed life-long friendships on the athletic fields. That's because in the smaller campus the students have the time to know each other. That has to help our program, too. These are friends blocking and tackling for friends.

Oh, don't get me wrong. I'd have loved a chance to sell a major school, too. If it has close proximity to a large metropolitan area, I'd be selling the availability of the very things we don't have at St. John's. I'd be pointing out the theaters, restaurants, availability of major industries and the enormous media coverage. I think I could sell the large school as well as the small. But my heart wouldn't be in it.

That's because I believe in what a smaller school can offer. The closeness of academia and students; the time to discuss problems with peers; the time to take a solitary stroll by the lake and just ponder your existence. These are basic things that sound so simple but are so difficult to find on a large campus.

I once told a recruit, "We are not numbers at St. John's. We are individuals — and we try to respect that." I try to spend as much time and get to know a third-string center as I do the starters. I think that after four years, I know all of my boys as well as a coach can. They may not think I have such a deep, personal interest in them, but I keep track of their grades, their family joys and problems, their job contacts and their progress after they leave school.

Gambling:

"The Art Schlicter gambling story troubled me. I kept saying that if he weren't a football player—say he was a truck driver—he'd never have been permitted to get in that kind of scandal."

One of them called me "Mannix" because I showed such interest in his affair with a young lady. Another said I reminded him of his dad. Another said I worked like a bloodhound. None of them seemed to mind and a steady stream of former players through my office and home is all the testimony I need that our caring is mutual.

How do you tell all these things to a recruit? You don't. If you are signing up a young man for football, remember three things:

1. Be sure your school is going to be his kind of school.
2. Be sure you have sold the academic program as hard as you have sold the athletic program.
3. Be sure he will understand that you care as much about him as a man as a football player.

If you satisfy yourself in those three areas, you have eventually turned out a decent, caring citizen. It's really that simple.

14
The Days of Decision and Turmoil

To every coach, particularly if you are successful, the day will come when the earth stands still: you will receive another offer.

Three times at St. John's I ran into moments of pride and agony which tore me up inside. For me the inner conflict began with the premise that if I can win at St. John's, I can win anywhere.

With that thought in mind, any coach will be receptive to offers. But I had another nagging belief — perhaps because I knew myself so well: I am not a company man. Oh, I can get along in a framework of organization and I don't throw rocks at the establishment. But I know that John Gagliardi teaches football that is considered "different." Not so much the game as the principles; not the execution, but the preparation.

My first feelings came in the 1950s when West Point was doing so much juggling with its Army football team. I could have hooked-on as head. I had watched Tyrone Power in the "Long Gray Line" on late-night TV as much as anyone. I could see myself on the sidelines, urging Tyrone on to great glory with generals like MacArthur and Eisenhower in the stands cheering me on. That's pretty heady stuff.

My wife, Peggy, one night sobered me up quickly: "You don't look good in gray, John."

More than that, the spit and polish of the mighty corps probably frightened me out of any dreams of being a super coach high above the Hudson. I guess that's because I am basically a live and let live guy. I have never had my team snap to attention. I have told you earlier that they come out of the huddle with the precision of a kindergarten ballet class. I have never really been heavy on dress codes. In fact, I had a championship team with four men festooned with full beards and I never really thought about it until somebody pointed them out on the team picture. Hell, as long as the beards didn't get in the way of their blocking and tackling, so what?

Long ago I learned about dress codes. I was taken aback when a young man appeared at post-dinner without a suit or sports coat. I mentioned it to him later and he explained, "I don't have one. Frankly, I haven't had the money." Enough said? I've always felt that if a young man can appear in church and the classroom, that same garb is good enough for football trips. Who am I to equate with God or professors? It's the neat mind I have come to admire — not necessarily the neat pants press.

So I asked myself: Army — with all its traditions, which I love, and all its discipline in minute areas, which I can't understand, will that make Gagliardi a complete, happy person? You know the answer before I say it.

The challenge of Notre Dame football and being asked to be interviewed by Ara Parseghian in the 1960s was much more gut-rendering.

Now here is a name that captures the magic and the mystique of the football world. Notre Dame! Is there a young coach who breathes who wouldn't be elated just to be considered for the Notre Dame staff? It's enough of an ego-pumper to make a coach believe he can indeed jump off seven-story buildings without harm.

For a week I agonized with my wife and close friends. Lord! Notre Dame! Parseghian! Not only to be a part of a great school and tradition but a coaching staff gleaned from the best all over the country. And Parseghian — a man equipped to become a legend. That is heady stuff.

My wife, Peggy, was, as usual, supportive. She once said, "Marry a football coach or a manufacturer's rep — what's the difference. Be prepared to travel." That's the kind of support I've had all my life.

I strolled the St. John's campus during the late October evenings, thinking: "Now is the chance, John. Now is the chance to get a national name on a major staff that is a proven winner. No doubt here. Notre Dame will win under Parseghian. Notre Dame coaches move out to head jobs all over the country in the glamor schools. The chance comes only once in a lifetime."

There was, at the same time, another voice. It kept saying, "John, is anything better than this? Oh sure, the money, the fame, the big-time headlines. But really, is there anything better than being head man, to call your own shots at a school that you really love?"

Marriage:

"When I married Peggy I promised her trips to enchanted lands. I took 40 years to get our first real vacation—and there I was looking at another job offer."

Try that on for size in the middle of the night when you wake up in a cold sweat. For five days I debated whether to at least make the move and look into the Notre Dame feeler. I was young enough to accept the risks. I was old enough to know that any move creates a little havoc in the home. I was stable enough to equate all the sides.

So one night I asked a few close friends over and put the questions to them: OK. Notre Dame — you know what that means. Instant recognition; the intangible every coach seeks. Also, a learning experience. Also, the chance to put a foot in the door of the big time. All positives, right. All my friends agreed.

What did they think were the points on the debit side of the ledger?

One said, "John, you're the big fish here — granted a smaller pond, but the people you teach here are every bit as important as the ones you'd be teaching at Notre Dame."

Another said, "Risk it . . . go ahead. Every coach has to move four or five times to prove his mettle and reach a true plateau. You have the guts and the skills — go for it; a once-in-a-century opportunity."

Then another man, whose instincts I dearly treasure, laid it on the line: "You'll never be happy being just a cog in the big wheel, John. You are a particularly unique individual. There's no place for individualists on a major staff. You'd shrivel up and die."

Too candid, you think? It struck home. "You are an individualist, John."

Dammit, I am. Perhaps too much so. Could an individualist subjugate himself for perhaps three or four years? On the other hand, authority can be opium to the senses. It might do me good, I thought, to work under another regime; it could be a magnificent lesson.

There were more sleepless nights. Was I an ogre who was so jealous of my own authority that I feared becoming a staff member? Would I continue to grow calling my own shots? Would I ever get a chance like this again? Would I ever be able to live with myself if I didn't experience the big time?

I waited another day. I asked another friend. He said, "The worst thing in the world, John, would be to wake up at the age of 60 and say, 'Why didn't I try the big time?' "

Wives:

"A football coach's wife must understand two things: for five months she might as well be married to a traveling salesman; and never plan a cocktail party after a game. After a loss, most coaches would prefer a solitary cell."

God, I was even more bewildered and gouged by anxiety. I prayed. I walked. I discussed it over and over with Peggy until she could be forgiven if she threw a bowl of cold chili in my lap.

Then a student said one day, "Hear a lot of rumors, Mr. Gagliardi. Hope they're not true."

It dawned on me. I was so zealous in my decision-making trauma I had actually turned selfish. I hadn't asked myself, "How about the seniors?" or "How about the St. John's program?"

I was only one small part of a splendid institution. I owed something to a school that had nurtured me in embryo coaching days. And maybe the guy who said I was an individualist was right. It would take some kind of a character to turn down an interview at Notre Dame.

I stayed. I felt good. About myself and the school and the players and the students. I said to myself, "Give it all you've got right here. This is a big enough challenge for anyone." I have continued to feel that way ever since.

* * * * * *

Nothing I had dealt with in the way of offers prepared me, however, for the 1983 episode. This time another small school — but in the palm-dotted, tropical paradise of San Diego — was at the doorstep. Another Catholic school. Another school with about the same modest ambitions and sports dimensions as St. John's. A very beautiful, comfortable place.

Now the reason this was the most enticing offer of all was not the prospect of football glory; no, it was because it came at a particular time of my life when every man sets his sights on retirement.

For instance, what better place to retire than San Diego with its nearly perfect weather? And the nine or 10 years I intend to coach — wouldn't that be a perfect time to get acquainted with the San Diego area? And a new challenge; the school did not have a particularly successful record and I'm sure its alumni must have a few ambitions of improvement. To be succinct, San Diego University officials said, "We want you. You are our kind of man."

Peggy and I decided to look into this one first hand. For nine magnificent days we were treated with respect and friendliness. The school, the campus, the students, the way of life was everything a coach could ask.

The 75 degree temperature was getting to me one night, when I said to Peggy at our hotel, "Let's flip a coin. Heads we take San Diego. Tails we go back to St. John's." The coin turned up heads.

I said, "Let's make it two out of three."

Peggy said, "This is going to be a tough one. Our children will be living and going to school in Minnesota. But you can't beat the weather. And the people have been wonderful."

The next day one of the hosts made a point of explaining what a paradise this would be for golf and tennis — daily. I don't play either.

That night another host wanted us to dine out on the terrace of a restaurant so we could see and hear the birds flying around more clearly. I whispered to Peggy, "I don't like feathers in my soup." She whispered back, "St. John's just scored another point."

I asked for a little time to think it over. On the plane I asked Peggy again, "Wouldn't I miss the pot holes in Minnesota?" She said, "Two points for St. John's."

God, was I getting too old to meet another challenge head-on? That fear grips you when you're in your 50s. Many times I had awakened the past few years to ask, "How much longer can I keep winning? The coaches in the league have my films for 30 years — they know me as well as I know myself."

But a friend pointed out, "John, you could lose every game for 10 years and still be over .500." That got my attention. But now I wondered if I had lost my guts — my willingness to try Gagliardi football in a new scheme.

I talked over the offer with St. John's officials. They were warm and responsive. They told me they respected any decision I would make, but that they hoped I would see fit to finish my career in Collegeville.

The day I turned down the offer I told Peggy, "This is it. I guess I'm a St. John's man. I believe too much in what we're doing here — I want to keep the fire going."

The reception by friends, family and alumni and St. John's academia was unbelievable. I received hundreds of letters and calls, expressing pleasure that I had decided to stay.

One letter particularly touched me. It said: "Mr. Gagliardi, I am so happy to have you stay on. We are devoted fans of St. John's football. My husband was prepared to sell his business and relocate in San Diego if you had moved."

That kind of loyalty is what life is all about.

I think all coaches at middle age are attacked with the furies. There are times you question whether or not the system is passing you by. You ponder when you might lose your effectiveness. You weary of the recruiting or the selling. But then you must grab yourself by the neck, look in the mirror and say, "Hell, I know more now than 25 years ago; I should know twice as much as those fast young guns coming up. I can show them the tough old warriors love new challenges."

Today I am happy and relieved by my decisions. Oh, there may be autumn evenings after a big victory when I will muse about what might have happened in West Point, South Bend or San Diego. But who has more than I have? Who has a warmer, nicer family than my St. John's family? Who has a better foundation on which to build — not just victories but worthwhile young people?

Fame or not; big college or not; win, lose or draw . . . I'm a very lucky man.

15
Little Things Count

It was a very wise lady who said, "No use puttin' up your umbrella until it rains."

I am constantly asked how the pressures on a winning coach affect his life. I am prone to answer facetiously, "Easier than those of a loser." But on second thought, that is not quite true. Learning to live with victories can be as difficult as learning to cope with losses. That's because always in the back of the mind is the nagging question: "When does the sour streak begin?"

Oh, yes. Every winning coach feels the strain . . . a great crop of players graduating . . . a super quarterback ends his career . . . a string of injuries suddenly wipes out a strong unit . . . the rivals get closer . . . they get smarter . . . they get more bold. It is always there, the spectre of defeat.

I have been fortunate to last so long that the paranoia of losing has lost a good deal of its grip. I have learned to fight back with humor, easing the work load, spending more time with my family. Then there is always the long walk in solitude.

I guess the best way to describe my approach to the psychology of winning is to say that every time my team has been defeated I was surprised. Think about that. I guess it tends to show that Old Gag always expects to win. I guess that is why I have been able to survive the strain and tensions of a competitive business; I never expect to lose it.'

Earlier I pointed out to you that it is of major importance to convey to your troops the feeling of complete confidence. Forget the odds. Forget the other side's supposed edge in manpower. Forget history. Imparting that belief and faith in winning is everything. And it must start from the coach.

Coaching is really a strange, fascinating profession. You can get up in the morning feeling confident, reflecting on a good practice the day before. Then you open the papers and read that unless your team plays over its head or stops the most deadly attack outside of germ warfare, you can't possibly win on Saturday. It has to make an imprint.

But I've always told my team that writers have a job to do; mainly create readership interest — or viewer ratings if they are sportscasters in televison. I tell them to forget what they read. Forget what they see. They know something that the media experts don't know: that St. John's will win on Saturday.

But where else in this life can you be convinced you are doing a strong, noble job and then read or hear from strangers that your team is not as capable as you believe. I once knew a coach who was mesmerized before each game by what he read in the papers or heard or saw on radio and TV. He was a veritable shambles by the end of the week.

"My God," he exclaimed to me, "I had no idea coaching included steeling yourself against the media. They didn't teach me that in coaching clinics."

Which brings up a very important and delicate point: the relationship you carve out with the media. I have a newsman as a close friend, and he told me, as a young man, that certain coaches were so arrogant and short-tempered he actually hated to ask a question for fear of being put down.

One scribe told me he felt that way about Woody Hayes who could be brusque. Another told me he virtually wilted in the presence of Bernie Bierman. I think this has to be a two-way street. A writer cannot feel intimidated by the coach and neither should a coach cower to a media person. Both are doing their job.

I notice lately that there seems to be a general critical atmosphere by media, perhaps a result of the intense competition. But I have known coaches who continually berate the press, such as Bobby Knight, and I feel that is a bad situation since the media need the team and the team needs the media to fill the seats.

Immortality:

"To become immortal, a football coach must have fine material, a lot of luck and a tremendous biographer."

I have often said it would be a pretty lonesome job if there were no fans shouting along the sidelines. I know my players and I would miss the headlines and the television features. One of the most rewarding parts of competition is to know your exploits are going to get recognition. I have long said that some of the great drives in men are for power, money — and recognition, and I am not so sure the latter might not be the most important.

Over the years I have gotten along well with the media. Oh, I've had my differences. One scribe used to be able to get under my skin in the way he phrased his questions. I had the feeling he wanted me to say what he wanted said. I finally told him, "Hey, don't keep twisting my words. I'll tell you anything you want to know, but let it come out my way." After that we got along famously.

There are a few scribes who aren't satisfied until they get you to knock somebody — the rules, officials, players, rival coaches, whatever. I learned long ago that amateur sports is no place to knock each other. I am constantly on the alert to try to give out praise. The language can be misunderstood easily enough without creating ill will.

I have been called a "cry baby" more than once for what one writer was "over-building" the rivals. But that's part of the game. It's fun. I know the other coaches do the same thing often when they refer to St. John's as being "a natural favorite because of all that tradition." It's only natural for me to get in the act and call my rivals, "The most under-rated force since David" or the "Sleeping giants . . . just waiting to be awakened." I don't think the war of words does much to psyche either team nearly as much as it sells a few more tickets. I firmly believe that college football is the best entertainment a dollar can buy. Why not sell it? Why not use the media and pep-up stories with some catchy quotes?

Not long ago we lost an important game and the rivals said they were hyped up by pasting up a column in the locker room written by a scribe who said St. John's would steamroller their team. Jokingly, I asked him if the other side hired him to write that. He made his point: "John, my words didn't beat you. It was a couple of blocks your guys missed." Absolutely right. For every team that's been steamed up by a media piece, there's one which made miserable mistakes because it was too high. This propaganda battle evens off.

I find that most media people are decent, hard-working professionals like ourselves. They must find news or create it or embellish it. Used properly, the media can be a giant force of good in promoting sports. We must have revenue. The media needs stories. Together, a chain of mutual benefit can be created.

I have been called a "terror" and a "cry baby" in regard to officials. One official refused ever again to work a St. John's game after my first season. I have heard that others have said the same thing. And let me be the first to admit that early on in my career I made some officials the scapegoat. Never to take blame from myself, but actually because I believed they made an error.

Perhaps I've mellowed a bit over the years, but I firmly believe a coach must show a little fire on the sideline. At least if a coach questions a few calls, the players know he's into the game — that the contest has his attention.

I remember sitting at a ball game as a youth and watching a close play at second base. The runner protested vehemently that he was safe. He threw down his cap, kicked dirt and screamed. But what made the impression on me was the fact his manager never did so much as get off his seat in the dugout. I thought, "Geeze, that must feel terrible — your own manager not coming out to protest a little, too." I vowed from that day on I'd question any controversial play.

Frankly, I don't know how much my eruptions for second-guessing on the sidelines has helped or hurt. One official told me, "John, I'll listen to you, but don't overdo it. Then I just get nasty."

In one game I lost control for a moment and shouted to a referee, "You stink!" He paced off 15 yards and shouted back to me, "How do I smell from here, Gag?" I had to smile.

There are times when my heart goes out to officials, too. There have been many miserable cold, wet, muddy days when their views were obliterated. When I come home particularly upset about a decision which might have cost us a game, Peggy will remind me, "You can't play without the officials, John." I've come to realize that down the years.

I once had a friend reprimand me for mouthing-off on the sidelines. After the game he asked me what my win record was and I said about 75 percent. He then reminded me, "You must have gotten a few fair calls along the way." He was right.

No coach can last without humor.

I always recall the story about the coach who developed such a persecution complex that every time the team went into a huddle, he thought the players were talking about him.

I've tried to maintain a sense of humor, particularly on the practice field.

I've always told my quarterbacks when I let them call signals that the six inches between their ears is the most valuable real estate in football. With a smile, I maintain the quarterback should call his own crucial plays because he's closer to the action than I am. But one young signal caller snapped back, "But John, you're the one that's getting paid!" Bravo.

One of our games was hit by a terrible deluge and the disappointed team looked around to see only a handful of fans. I told the players, "Don't get upset. Today we're going to try something new — we're going to introduce the fans to the players." The young men howled in glee.

I tell my men about the halfback who asked his girl to watch him practice, and then asked the coach if he could circle end to show her his speed. He did and was promptly hit by a linebacker who happened to catch him at the waist and dragged his pants down to his knees. The boy was embarrassingly trying to cover up and the coach shouted, "That's OK, fellow — it's the only good showing you made all season!"

One astonished youngster questioned us about our lack of equipment in drills. When I explained our philosophy, he cracked, "Gee, we'll really wallop anybody who shows up for a game with no pads on."

Football is made for humor. Grab it and savor it.

I remind the players about the quarterback being upset because his coach, like me, won't call the tough plays. The coach was ready: "Hey, you're on a four-year scholarship. I have a one-year contract. You call it."

I asked one of our young frosh if he thought he was quick or fast? "Just scared," came the honest reply.

At St. John's we have tried to blend humor with the serious business of preparation. One day a little fire started in my office and I was complaining that it had burned out a few play-cards. One player grinned, "Took a fire to get you to come up with some new stuff, eh?"

A professor told me he had really gotten tough on a student for doing sloppy work in his class. He lashed out at the young man and then, later, apologized for perhaps being a little too harsh. "That's OK," the young man explained, "I'm used to having people lay it on me. I'm the second string quarterback."

One day I shocked a few of my players by telling them I hoped they weren't good sports. One of them asked, "How come, John?" And I pointed out that you have to lose to prove you're a good sport.

I like to tell my team about the little boy who kept taking a dollar to the candy store, getting change, and then converting it back into a dollar bill at the bank. Somebody asked him why. "Well, some day somebody's going to make a mistake and it ain't going to be me." I tell them that's how I want us to play. Do our thing. When the mistakes are made, they're going to be made by the other team.

On dress codes, I always say only, "Look neat and smell good." A new player heard this and said, "I suppose Gag's football instructions are just simple: carry ball — run far."

I loved coaching track. My only advice was: "Get in front and stay there."

You have to have a grin now and then on the gridiron. This isn't life and death. But too many coaches in their confrontations with the media and players make it that way.

You can always tell the coaches whose insides won't take it long when you observe the dinner table at clinics. They are the ones drinking milk — usually protecting an ulcer.

I don't play golf or tennis for recreation. But I find time to read, walk, listen to the children and get into town once or twice a week for lunch with alumni and friends.

I've coached long enough to say it's a wonderful profession if you stay out of turmoil. Napoleon said he'd rather face the enemy in battle than read the headlines in the morning papers.

Coaches have to learn to face the enemy on the field of strife, digest the headlines and put on a smile.

16
Unlikely Heroes Are St. John's Legacy

An "unlikely" hero is simply a man who rises to the occasion when given a special assignment which can make or break a game plan. They abound in St. John's lore. It's not so much that they are household words, rather they reflect that spirit which seems to identify with St. John's victories — an electric, vital contribution by someone from out of the ranks.

I remember while coaching high school football in Colorado we played a game against a small, fast foe. They did have a remarkably large tight end who was averaging over five pass receptions a game. He'd also be switched to running back on certain occasions down near a foe's goal line for sheer power. He was averaging over four yards a carry on size alone.

Jokingly, I asked for volunteers to match this giant. A 150-pound reserve linebacker volunteered. I told him we didn't need any suicides, just a good defender. The young man insisted. The squad wanted him to get a chance. One of our regulars was injured and so I said, "OK — but try not to get hurt. You're giving away over 60 pounds." He looked at me and said, "This is my chance. I want it!"

Well, the inexperienced young man was assigned to cover the giant regardless of where he went. On the first play he was called for interference. On the second pass, he was stung for a 20-yard gain. But on the third pass to the tall foe, he timed his jump perfectly and knocked the ball away cleanly. When the game had wound its course, the inexperienced little sophomore had limited the giant tight end to three receptions for just 42 yards — had intercepted one pass and knocked down five others. He also tackled the big boy twice for losses when he carried the ball. In desperation, the big fellow threw the ball at our defensive nemesis, donating us 15 yards.

In the end, a 150-pounder had whipped a 220-pounder by courage and desire and the grit to impress the coach. Never again was I afraid to put a small man head-on-head with a bigger foe.

Never had St. John's enjoyed an unlikely hero more than Steve Setzler who made it with the 1973 San Francisco 49ers. He was a big, gawky young man from the St. John's preps. No blue-chipper he, just a walk-on. For two years Steve struggled as a tight end — an average second team performer. He didn't appear to have the speed, finesse or coordination to become a standout, but one day he got his break: a middle guard was injured and I asked Steve if he'd switch positions. He answered, "I'll go anyplace I can play." He had never played middle guard, which can be a tough, punishing position.

How well did Steve do? Well, he was drafted by the 49ers and went on to play with the New York Stars in the World Football League.

Steve left me puzzled about myself. I kept asking, "Why can't I recognize talent like that sooner? It troubled me until somebody pointed out that perhaps Steve never would have made it at tight end. But it proves how often luck plays such a vital role in making an unlikely hero.

Attitude:

"At St. John's the right attitude just means that a player is willing to play any position at any time."

Steve, however, had an inherent gift you couldn't tell without X-ray eyes: he had a blue-chip heart. I wish there was some way we could diagnose the players with intestinal fortitude. Steve didn't show his true qualities until the pressure was on. Nobody did better under fire. He had instincts that were brought out only, it seemed, in the big game; particularly the big play. He could virtually smell the ball carrier's scent. Pro scouts loved his ability to react instinctively. Yet, he was a walk-on.

Another unlikely St. John's grid hero was the magnificent little 128-pounder Bill Laliberte. Yes, I said 128 pounds. He became the leading rusher in the conference. He was a standout blocker; an all-state man who looked as if his uniform might fall off his small frame. He led us to the 1969 Mineral Water Bowl title and was heralded as the most valuable player.

I still show recruits and even our veterans films of this remarkable little man running and blocking. And the punch line: he was never hurt. From that moment on, I never asked myself, "Is that player big enough?" Only, "Is he good enough?"

I recall, however, that I did listen to his prep coach, Irv Nerdahl of Robbinsdale, Minnesota. He told me, "John, some day that little fellow will start for you." I had reservations. When he landed at St. John's, he barely tipped the scales at 120 pounds.

Defensive starter Jim Kruzich, who is now an attorney, said that he taught himself to believe at St. John's that there was nothing the man across from him could do that he couldn't neutralize. He was not that mobile, but he became a standout. Another unlikely hero who learned to believe.

I will give this word of advice once more to young coaches: never pre-ordain that a man is too small, too slow or too clumsy. There are many heroes today who need only the chance.

Who can forget John Ringle, who knocked pro-to-be Barry Bennett down 36 times in a pair of 49-0 and 31-0 victories over Concordia. He was outweighed by nearly 30 pounds. Ringle told me after those achievements that, "It made me feel as though I could accomplish anything in life." He'd never feel like an underdog again.

CELEBRATING THE 1976 NATIONAL CHAMPIONSHIP at the Washington, D.C. Touchdown Club, top right, is John Gagliardi. Among the other guests: Joe Campbell, Tony Dorsett, Elroy Hirsch, Bruce Jenner, Jack Kemp, John Madden, Sugar Ray Leonard, Bob Feller, Ken Stabler and Roger Staubach.

I remember Ringle's blocks as if they were yesterday; low and devastating. He was impatient with himself if he didn't sprawl a few 200-pounders every game. They became his prime target. You can't believe how that makes a coach feel — to see a young man believing.

I still show new players films of Ringle's amazing talent for cutting monster players down to size.

Oh, the Johnny grid pages are filled with unlikely heroes. How about Little All-American Joe Kiley of Owatonna, Minnesota? He rode the bench for two years. Finally, an injury to a starter put Joe into the battle. He wasn't that big, only 195 pounds for a defensive end. But he soaked up coaching and he had the Johnnies' feel for the action. And he believed.

I saw him surge in to harass passers and leap and power through the blockers to collar breakaway backs. This man was a substitute who saw no action until his junior year. His improvement was incredible. Every game he became smarter and more difficult to block. Every game he found new ways of confusing the offensive men assigned to him. What we didn't teach him, he created. What he didn't have the size to accomplish, he made up for in agility and balance and being in the right place. By his senior year I wouldn't have traded him for any defensive man in the country.

In fact, he got so good I had to question my own observation values. I mean here I had an All-American on the bench. All he needed was the chance. But to be truthful, I'd have rated him an unlikely hero while he was a substitute.

Future:

"Funny how many poor football players become exceptional in their various careers. When I think of that, I realize how trivial blocking and tackling is in life."

I might embarrass the man, but I remember another unlikely hero. We'll call him Stan. Anyway, Stan told me he had a fear of being hurt and was thinking about quitting the squad. It was strictly a mental thing. But one day I sat with him for nearly an hour and pointed out how few serious injuries we had suffered over the years. I told him it was a fear he must conquer to become a success at anything he did. Fears have a tendency to multiply.

Stan agreed to take a chance and we put him in as a reserve pass defender. After a tentative appearance in the first couple of games, he made a resounding tackle you could hear all over the stadium. Both players laid on the ground for several seconds. I thought, "Oh, oh! Stan got it on his first big play." But he got up, and the rival stayed down, and then he turned toward me with a big grin.

He nodded as if to say, "Hey, I made it. I'm all in one piece." But the strange thing is, by admitting his fear and conquering it, Stan became an outstanding secondary and open field hitter. He leveled foes for two years and went on to all-conference honors. He also carried his bravery over into the war and was decorated.

It goes back to Teddy Roosevelt of the Rough Riders. The playing fields and gyms made strong, brave men; the kind that can serve family, country and God.

I think unlikely heroes have a chance to excel at St. John's because we respect the intellect as much as the muscle. We want people who can think; men who can work out problems in their minds and carry them over to the grid.

I had one young fellow who told me, "I really never liked football but my dad always pushed me. But just getting in a couple of games has made me believe you can learn something from anything you do. In fact, you should try some things you might not like. I think I've gained from football because of the give and take."

Ironically, that boy went on to become a whale of a baseball player, getting a minor league contract. He later told me the lessons of trying to make a team in a sport he didn't like actually gave him the fortitude to play minor league baseball with its dusty bus trips and second-rate hotels.

Knute Rockne once said of surprise heroes, "They are the young men who don't know what they have inside until that big play comes. Then they rise to the occasion and sometimes they fool even themselves."

I think the only difference between the unlikely hero and the man who is groomed for the key role is that the one player has to dig down and test himself and may be a bit surprised at what he finds. The man who expects to perform well is used to it and has felt like a leader from the cradle. The unlikely hero is a man who performs better than he believes he can.

I think our high ratio of the unlikely hero at St. John's is due in part to the fact we have never had that many blue-chip players. Or rather, we didn't have that many performers that other college scouts considered blue chip. We got men who could think, could adapt and improve and were coachable. They just needed the proper tuning.

It's like the guy who claims to hate snails until he accidently consumes them in an elaborate buffet and never realizes it until two days later when somebody asks him how he liked them. "Great," he explains sheepishly. The unlikely hero finds himself feeling "great" because he's found something he likes — himself.

17
The Anguish of a Losing Streak

At any age when I should have been completely comfortable with my role as a veteran coach, I was suddenly caught in the avalanche: three straight losses to open the 1983 campaign. I can't blame them on a rebuilding year; we had plenty of seniors. I can't blame it on complacency since our squad never concentrated harder. In the end I could blame it on my own judgment: not being able to pick the best 22 players.

I think it happens to all coaches. I opened with a blend of 11 seniors on the first 22. That would give us great stability and dedication. I figured I had enough experience to handle most early season problems.

But my ball of twine began to unravel in the first game when we lost a heartbreaker. Then we got soundly trounced in the second game, and I began to make changes which I probably hadn't implemented in 20 years. I began to move in some gifted sophomores and freshmen, and when we were beaten a third straight time, I completed the overhauling by inserting seven new men into the two platoons by the fourth game.

Those were disheartening days. I began to wonder if it were possible to lose 70 straight. I don't care if you have a 10-year mark of 80% victories, the day comes when you question your ability. Remember, there is always someone out there who can beat you. I have never known an astute coach who didn't have a certain degree of humility because all of us have taken it on the chin.

I said to myself one forlorn afternoon, "God, John, if Knute Rockne could lose three games in a season and if Bo Schembechler can be beaten regularly in bowl games and if Don Shula and Bud Grant can be hammered, why feel badly about losing a few?" That kind of thinking helped — but not for long.

First, it is a terrible thing — the worst in coaching — to have to tell fine young men who have waited and drilled two or three years for a chance to make the first team that they are not gifted enough. I know it must be a terrible blow to their morale. I try to explain that football at St. John's is a complete team sport; we must look at it that way and since the team is losing, something has to be done. I thank them all for their loyalty and tell them they still have a chance to retain a spot on the starting team if my changes don't work out.

I think it is a tribute to St. John's team dedication that not one youngster in over 30 years has complained about being demoted.

The trouble with all of us coaches is that too often we put experience ahead of talent. Since we carry such large squads at St. John's, it is true that sometimes it takes longer for me to assess the gifted athlete than I might with a smaller squad. But it is also true that because of the size of our squads, we probably give more hope to more athletes over a longer period of time.

Anyway, the changes began: A freshman quarterback and eventually a freshman running back and sophomore runner. A couple of new, young, defensive men. A pair of offensive linemen out of the ranks. A couple of more moves on special teams.

I had to find people who believed — but more importantly, I had to find people who could execute. I told the players who had not produced, that new men would replace veterans until we found execution. But secretly, I wondered to myself if I had lost my touch. There were nights I had trouble sleeping. There were meals left uneaten. There were times when I wanted to be alone and there were times I wondered if I was over-rated. I wondered if I had lost my zest for battle.

Any veteran coach will tell you how humbling this experience is. I had just turned down an offer and decided to remain at St. John's. The school was so generous in support of me and the program that I felt I was driving a stake through its heart. I would look at the stories about my decision to stay and shake my head. Maybe it would have been better for St. John's if I left.

Gradually I saw a change in execution and in practice. The timing seemed to flow and the plays seemed to crack and snap. I don't know if it was the infectious enthusiasm of the freshmen or the pent-up emotion that young players can generate when they want to turn the situation around, but I know the Johnnies were ready to explode. At least, I hoped I hadn't imagined all this during drills.

But we did bounce back — with such an astonishing rush I was even boggled. The blocking improved, the tackling pursuit soon looked like days of old. I saw freshmen taking on leadership qualities. Our special teams began to strike with precision and tenacity.

Coaching:
"Being a good coach demands the same qualities as being a good parent."

Soon we were on a roll — and before it ended in post-season play to a fine Duluth team, we had reeled off seven straight victories. We had found a splendid new passer in Rick Daugherty, a freshman with the heart of a lion. We took a bad beating in his first few games before he began to read the defense — but he stood up under the punishment. Some day he will be one of the finest passers in the nation. But more, he is a leader and a tremendous competitor who finished among the top three in our division nationally with his completion ratio of over 60 percent.

Another freshman, Vince Reiter, became a slashing, hard-hitting runner. He had no fear. He must have averaged over five yards per carry down the stretch and has excellent speed in an open field. Young rookie Dan DeClouet, rated third in the nation in our division on punt returns, can become an electrifying performer.

Suddenly, everywhere I looked I had new, fresh, ambitious prospects.

What I love most about our newcomers is that they didn't come to St. John's asking, "Who's ahead of me? How long before I become a starter?" They just went out and earned it. They stood in the shadows of a huge squad, but before the season was one-third old, their gifts had been discovered. I don't take credit for that. Perhaps I should have found them sooner. But I want to drive home the point that adversity is not only the mother of discovery, but it belies that old saw about the "over-achiever."

You know what people say about some youngsters, "Oh, they are over-achievers; they just have to excel." That's nonsense, I believe. I say they're just gifted people who need the chance; people who believe in themselves. They are the ones who want to succeed. They are not "over-achieving," just fulfilling their capabilities when they get the chance.

I eventually thanked God for the season. It could have been a disaster. You coaches know what I mean. There is always the time when you look in the mirror and ask yourself, 'Have I lost it? Am I failing to communicate? Have I fallen behind the times?' I am sure Bear Bryant had those days when he lost eight of 10 bowl bowl games, but he kept coming back because he had a faith in himself and his system.

I learned something else from this season. I know I have repeated in this book many times the importance of stability and believing. But also, the coach owes it to his squad when he is losing to search out the rest of the squad. Look for some bright-eyed, ambitious youngster who maybe doesn't have the natural gifts or experience, but who wants to play and owns the big heart. Remember: you can't test the heart of his combative skills until he is in the lineup.

As I look back, it was heart-searing to have to demote some fine young men. But they came to St. John's to become involved in the glory and success of their school on all levels. They recognized that the losing could not go on and that they had ample time to turn the situation around. In the end, we needed new men who could make the entire force work better as a unit. Thankfully, we found it without tinkering all season. Some teams never find the right combination. But I assure you, I would rather go down the drain shuffling the deck of cards than standing with a pat hand and taking loss after loss.

In the end, we would up with seven seniors, nine juniors, four sophomores and three freshmen among our top 23 players. We also unveiled another three or four freshmen who had the ability to move into the ranks with confidence and high spirits the following fall. We found a good kicking game, solid special teams and a balanced run-pass game which averaged nearly 400 yards per game down to the wire.

From being mired in disappointment and berating myself early in the year, I climbed out of the pits with a smile on my face, feeling that I had dared to make moves and dared to unmask new talent and dared to experiment. Frankly, during the early losses, I had questioned whether I would dare do anything except sit back and hope. The new moves did more than win; they strengthened my faith in my ability to comb the squad for new talent that could get the job done.

I think all of us at one time or another are guilty of standing pat. We begin to perform consistently at a high level plateau. When we are jarred, we don't react with our instincts; we play too often by the book, hoping that the percentages gained will take over.

Dare to make some moves. I have complete faith in our system here of gradually working the experienced men in. But there comes a time when even experience must give way to raw talent, even if that talent is carried by a pink-cheeked freshman just out of high school.

Because of the changes I was forced to make — and which really hurt me deeply — I could welcome the next few years, anticipating the maturing of the gifted sophomores and freshmen. Oh, I know enough about life, football injuries and transfers to know nothing is beyond surprise and disappointment. But if the group finally welded continues to improve and remains healthy, I can truthfully again look forward to challenging for national titles.

I know I have talked so much about success begetting success and momentum cascading into more momentum, but please, I hope everyone learns from my losing experience. Because I lost, I again craved the zest of winning. Because I got whipped, I wanted more than ever to feel the joys of victory. Because our team was beaten, it wanted more than ever to justify its ambition and dedication.

Thank God for defeats. They stimulate and infuse and drive a man to goals he might not attain were it not for the setbacks.

What they say about Gag:

"He taught me to believe in myself — to believe you can be a winner. Gag has a way of giving you complete confidence. There is always a solution to the problem. I remember the feeling that, 'Gosh, if we lose, it would be a terrible shock.' You don't expect to lose with Gagliardi. He is more than a master coach, he is a master psychologist. The Big Red line permeates some part of you all your life.

"I remember a big 40-10 homecoming victory and I privately commented to John, 'What a boring game.' John laughed and said, 'Father, if you want just entertainment, try a variety show.' You hear that nobody ever tackled anyone at St. John's. Well, you tackled in your mind. From Gag, you got the feeling of pride and also that you could never trust a man from St. Thomas. I have to laugh. I still feel uneasy around Tommies."

—Mike Perry

"He taught you to hang together — pride in yourself and the team. I can remember him asking, 'Why tackle each other? Tackle is just desire and you don't have to practice desire. It's either with you or not.' He is the kind of coach who had us drawing up plays with our fingers in the dirt. The real grass roots game. Gag simplified everything. He made a complex game easy for young players. He is a master of basics. He exuded confidence — that ability to make all around him believe. It has to have helped every man who played for him in his future life."

— Peter Rockers

THE ENTIRE GAGLIARDI FAMILY celebrates John's decision to stay at St. John's after he received a tempting offer from San Diego University.

"I admired him as a fine coach. But it wasn't until I was graduated that the strength and wit and humility of John Gagliardi really struck home. We are better friends today than when I played for him. So many other Johnnies tell me the same thing. That is a vital aspect of this fine leader: you want to be his friend long after you've played for him. I get a good feeling to go back and talk to him every few months. His values and trust are very important things in my life."

—Tom Schutta

"As an official I saw Gagliardi explode and I've seen him be passionate. I always had the feeling that no coach in the country was more up on the game — into it so thoroughly. He could be a wild man and that tongue could lash out. But I've seen him apologize if he was wrong and I've seen him compliment officials. He has made a terrible reputation in some quarters with his tirades against officials. But Billy Martin and Leo Durocher and Earl Weaver did the same thing with umpires and earned Hall of Fame status. Gag is simply a great coach who will fight for every decision. Every whistle to him is vital."

—Jim Griffith

"I'm just a fan who is completely turned on to Gagliardi's style. My son played against his teams. But I always admired the organization, the purpose, the instincts that seemed to be behind St. John's football. With Gag, it seemed the unexpected became the expected. No fan's dollars ever bought them more entertainment — quality entertainment — than watching St. John's red machine. St. John's football is Gagliardi football. And it's apparent it's a winner."

—Don Gervais

"I don't know of a coach who so implanted his philosophy on a team from the first day of practice. I continually hear former Johnnies quoting passages from Gagliardi's speeches. He has a way of giving them something they always carry. He has a way of putting football in the proper perspective; an important game — but just one factor in life. I used to double date with John and Peggy. I can tell you his deep, dedicated interest in people goes far beyond the field of football. He is a magnetic individual who has learned to handle life's emotions with stability and foresight."

—Dan Brutger

"I fell in love with Gagliardi's concepts the first time I heard him speak as a freshman at the Shanley High School prep football dinner. First, he had a great sense of humor. Then he showed compassion. Finally, he showed enthusiasm and sound philosophy. I knew he cared about his players. I made up my mind in high school that I had to play for that man. And it was ironic: in our Shanley system with its great winning tradition, discipline was a major share of the program. At St. John's the pace was easy and out-going, but I got fully as much out of one as the other. Gagliardi knows how to make football fun — as well as how to win."

—Charlie Hanish

"I learned competitiveness from Gagliardi. I learned that battling your way through the big St. John's squads is like life; you can get there if you work at it. I learned from Gagliardi that it's better to win than to lose. I took a job after graduation where I hit the streets and it was tough. But everything I learned about pride and devotion and staying at it until you win, helped me in my job. I led my group in sales the first year and every day something happens that makes me reflect back on Gag and on his St. John's program. I think he truly is one of life's greatest winners in all departments."

—Lou Raiola

"From Gag I learned that you can smile under duress; that you can innovate and that you can apply football to everyday career action. He's one in a million — whether falling over desks trying to explain a play or running through crazy fun-drills in shorts. There's a method to his madness; it's called instilling confidence. This man puts football in its proper perspective: another part of your education. On the field or off, Gag is a teacher — a very inspirational one."

—Joe Cascalenda

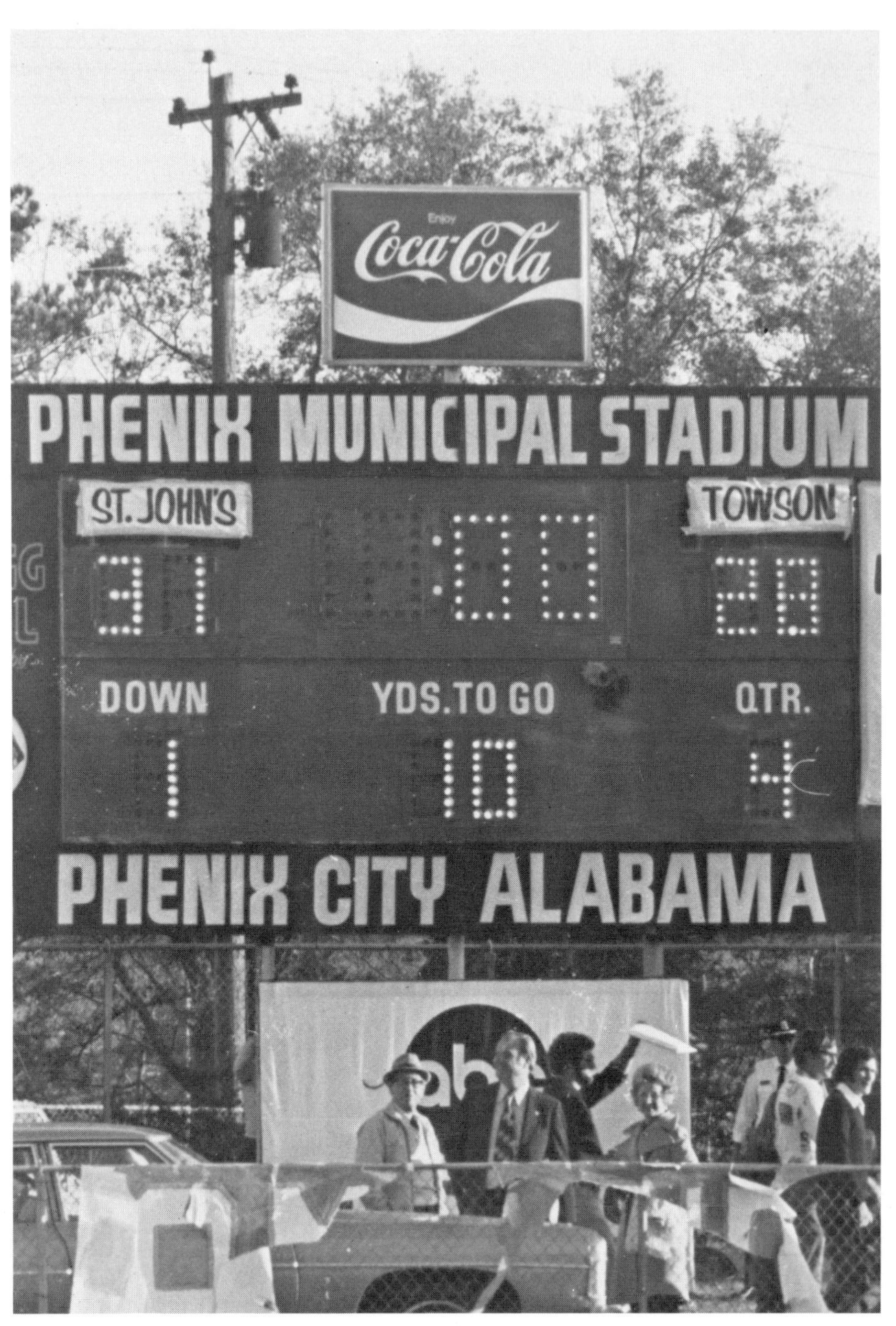

THE SCOREBOARD TELLS IT ALL after the Johnnies won the thrilling national championship in 1976 in Alabama.

18
Reflections on Coaches, Losing and Other Things

I suppose all of us have our idols in the coaching field. From Knute Rockne's letters and books, I learned that he was probably the most inspirational force to ever appear on the college football scene.

From Bear Bryant I learned the great ones are marked by adaptability. He went through so many changes, including the wishbone offense. He went through integration. The man's longevity proved he could change — and that's so hard for many coaches.

I constantly reflect on Vince Lombardi's greatness. His devotion to the game is what, I think, marked him as a legend. Nobody moved football to a higher plane of endeavor. Lombardi was a master.

I am a close and loyal admirer of Bud Grant of the Vikings. His complete control of his emotions during a game was unbelievable. He's taught me to do the thing you believe in. Plus, I love the fact he doesn't take himself that seriously. Grant represents level-headedness at its best.

I think that a coach must continually reinforce his thinking. I think he must constantly strive for impeccable image. Now we know that isn't attainable — we are too full of human frailties. But I think if a coach can get young people looking at him and admire him as we all did, say, John Wayne, that is the spirit of loyalty and courage that I think young people can commit themselves to.

I am often asked what makes the black athlete so thunderously successful. I believe they have hungrier genes — or in other words, more desire. They are fighting, in many instances, to improve their way of life. I have not had the opportunity to coach as many as I would like. I am disappointed about that.

Great athletes are the ones who believe they can be great — not necessarily the ones with the most physical attributes. I sat down one day and figured out that if I had judged my football players merely on their natural skills, I would have missed out coaching at least 12-15 all-conference performers. I think it is more wise to look at the eyes — rather than the muscles.

* * * * * *

I feel uneasy at coaching clinics. I have the feeling they expect me to give them a bonafide, guaranteed way of winning. I prefer to tell them how I win —

and hope they can glean something out of it. Nobody can adapt completely another coach's formula. You must first try to understand his philosophy, then transport it to the practice field. You may have a completely different way of getting your points across than the other man. A team is stamped by the coach. Every coach has his own technique, his own ideas, his own way of motivation. When I go to a clinic, I don't look for plays; I try to search out ideas. Fresh ideas make a clinic worthwhile. Nothing that is put on the blackboard hasn't been there many times before.

* * * * * *

Certainly I have an empty gut feeling when I lose. And there are people who say I am the absolute worst dinner companion after a defeat. But I do try each year to put the loss out of my head as quickly as possible. I'll tell you a good way to handle a loss: simply accept it as a learning experience. I try to learn a lesson from each loss. But don't ever dwell on it for more than a few hours. After a particularly bad beating, I may not even show the movies to the team. Begin looking ahead almost immediately. If every general who ever lost a battle didn't shake it from his mind, no war would ever have been won.

The greatest thing about my position at St. John's is the complete freedom; in a way, I am my own boss. Now that can cause a problem if you're too easy on yourself. But, by being athletic director, I get caught up in all phases of our sports program — from finding jerseys for the Bennies to ordering helmets. If you have any leaning toward the feeling of power and stature, try talking to the plumber about leaky showers or how to get grass stains out of your pants.

* * * * * *

I can't understand how coaches at the so-called football factories can absolve their conscience from not insisting and aiding an athlete to graduate. And as quickly as possible. I'm happy that I'm in a school where scholastics come first. If I thought we were just using football players to motivate our sports program, I'd get out of coaching in a minute. I guess that's one underlying reason why I was never that enthusiastic about a major job. I felt if they wanted me to build a winner and would pay a large salary, that football must be more important than English literature. There is comfort in knowing virtually every football player I have coached has been graduated. That, and the fact that only a handful ever left our program with a nagging injury. Football, no matter how important to the man, is not worth ruining a young man's health.

* * * * * *

When young men ask me to judge how much it will take to make them happy, I recall Richard Burton and tell them that at one time he had a 100-foot yacht, a twin engine jet, $5 million and Liz Taylor. But he always looked sad and never seemed to be able to find stability. Happiness is finding your niche — no matter what size — and doing your best with the tools that God gave you. If I measured happiness and satisfaction in monetary terms, I'd have never lasted two years in this profession.

I know so many coaches who play golf. I suppose I should have taken it up. But I always had the feeling I was wasting time — just out there in the pretty scenery, walking around. But I admire golfers who can put their problems aside for a few hours. That's smart. Sometimes I'd like to take a sea cruise, too. I just don't know if I can trust myself with so much leisure.

* * * * * *

I have often said that stupidity kept me alive. I have so often been unable to recognize the true strength of teams, as in post-season play. But perhaps that is God's gift to me. If I recognized the other team's talent, I would worry; the worry would reflect on my coaching and the coaching would reflect on our team performance. I guess the truth is: I just don't want to know how good the other side is.

You can say that perhaps that is running away from life. Or is it? If I don't dwell on rivals' stats and personnel, I am working longer on our plan. I am working longer on building up our confidence. If you study the other side too closely, you may find them influencing your own perspective. I never felt I had the luxury of being able to know as much about my rival as I did about my own team.

* * * * * *

My idea of innate competitive class is the man who can fight his way back against the flow to make the big play. Sometimes it's God-given instinct. Sometimes it is an animal fury. Mostly, it's just damn admirable competitiveness.

* * * * * *

Getting back to losing, which is something I hate to do: From the time the cave men sought to discover fire, I suppose man has been on the quest for victory. It is a natural instinct — otherwise the human race would never have improved.

Let's face it: there is more failure than success in all sports. Let's take track men. I would say that not more than 10 percent of the time are they happy with their performances. Even a victor may be disappointed in his time. We have to learn to live with losses. And winning teams can be unhappy because they didn't play that well.

Only twice in my career have I lost three games in a row. That happened recently. Now, despite the overwhelming victory percentage for St. John's, I was beginning to wonder. I knew I'd have to lose 157 straight to fall below .500 and was beginning to wonder if that was going to be the case.

Imagine! At my age and with all the experience, I could still sustain self-doubts. That has to be human nature. We have to live with the realization that in so many sports the failure is just around the corner. I so admire 7,000 marathon runners when they know only one will win. Thirty-two cars chase the Indy 500 winner. You have to be so happy to succeed more than you fail. To survive in the hectic world of sports — as rewarding as they are — you have to have a perspective that permits you to absorb disappointment.

I think two true masters of the art of riding the unpredictable punches of the football scene are former Minnesota coach Bud Grant and Don Shula of Miami. Both have accepted the fact that defeat is a part of the game. Neither tortures himself with a loss. Shula has told me that perhaps he has mellowed with age. But he can now look at the overall perspective and see that winning cannot be sustained no matter how hard you work.

After losing a 21-14 game in 1983, I felt we had given it away. The team that opened our losing streak — St. Cloud — turned out to be a fine, nationally-ranked club, but we still lost because of mistakes. It hurts to lose that way. The second week we were whipped badly by Hamline University. I knew then we didn't deserve to be ranked among the title contenders. The third week, St. Thomas overwhelmed us in all departments. But we found a freshman quarterback — and suddenly the old heart skips a beat and you start looking ahead again.

I also made nine changes out of the top 22 men in that last string of setbacks. Now that can hurt the morale of a team. I had to do it. That's like telling a salesman he's fired because the whole sales team hasn't hit the quota. But you have to try something. I finally got the team turned around — but I hate shuffling for the sake of ending a losing streak. I learned great empathy for the colleges that are struggling.

In restrospect, we ran into three fine football teams and we faced them in our rebuilding years. But it does tear you up inside — and I found, even after all the years, there are pangs and pains. Self-doubt will always be with us, but it is the strong man and coach who turns that self-doubt into confidence. Accept the challenge. I feel the losing strings, as rare as they have been, taught vital lessons of self-will and self-determination; they make you look at yourself and examine your philosophy.

Always remember: you can be tougher on your team when you win than when you lose. Remember, too: they are hurting, too.

* * * * * *

On the matter of easy openers, I remember Al McGuire, when he coached Marquette basketball, always saying: "I prefer to open at home against East Cupcake State." But today in football it becomes difficult to pick breathers, although I believe a first game victory stimulates confidence, and a strong performance at home early can be vital to a season.

The question I have been asked most often is, "What ingredients, if you pick the ideal core of a team, would you want?" I have to say speed and aggressiveness. You flounder without them. Also the quarterback. Today, he is essential. Take away a top quarterback, the speed and the fury, and no coach can win. All the emotion and desire and confidence cannot consistently offset the lack of speed, which is what exploits the openings and gives you the long-range striking force. No matter the coaching, without an adaptable, flexible quarterback you are beating your head against the wall.

* * * * * *

A former coach turned businessman told me, "The difference in coaching and business is that the thrills — the highs and the lows — are not nearly as great. Security is there — but it's not as fun." I recall our loss after 23 straight wins; it was plummeting into an abyss. The higher you are, the longer the fall.

That's why I keep looking ahead preaching victory, contemplating tomorrow. If you lose, look up. If you are on a high — keep striving. The truth is we are all looking for the secret of success, paradise — but let's never overlook or harden ourself to feeling compassion for the strugglers. On top, it's easy to philosophize and be brave.

I feel sports should be a proud profession and we should never laugh or criticize the masses who build sports heroes. The heroes take their minds off the grind of everyday problems; the tension that jobs and family troubles build.

Remember this, coaches: the day you quit or are fired, there are hundreds who would love to fill your shoes. Sports provides the great release for millions of human emotions. I say we are the warriors of our nation. There are only a handful of heroes. It's great to be that hero, but his time passes. The one thing that never passes; the need for the public to create sports celebrities and share in our game.

* * * * * *

Every coach I suppose gets heavy-hearted at times wondering just how important his job is. I feel that way, too. Then, when I have a slight dip in self-worth, I recall that sports pages are read almost four to one over editorial pages. That has to tell you that, for the majority of people, sports holds a vital position in their span of interests. If four times as many people are concerned about football than the economy, I guess we can say coaching is a pretty vital and responsible position.

I love to be able to tell a quarterback, "Ted, you call the play. You're my field leader." Sometimes the look of wonderment is astonishing. I have had young men tell me that, when they called their own play in a tough situation, it gave them an assurance that lasted well into their careers. Now, isn't that what coaching is all about?

I feel sorry for the big-time coaches who are primarily concerned only with turning out a winner and filling the stadium with mercenary players who don't know the school song. Lord, I have to believe that instilling in your men confidence to call their own plays, confidence to make judgments and confidence to move a shade in one direction or the other is the primary purpose of coaching this game.

"GREAT WORK, HONEY, I'M SO PROUD OF YOU," admiring wife Peggy says during John's 1983 testimonial.

We're trying to develop leadership — not stifle it. That's why I can't understand why coaches so frequently have taken the procedure of choice away from the athlete. If he can't make his own decision on a football field, how is he going to make it in the complexities of raising a family and creating a career?

* * * * * *

What the public will never know is that the bull elephant has many scars to show for his success.

Postscript

THE WHOLE CLAN gathers to celebrate another national championship.

What Peggy Gagliardi Says About Gag

"After spending 27 years with John, I have come to realize that he is a three-faceted man. First, he is a family man. That takes precedence over all else with him, it seems to me.

"Secondly, he is a successful coach. And third, he is a recognized figure.

"John enjoys spending time with his family. This is the most important part of his life. He also enjoys his close friends.

"After 40 years in coaching he has players all over the world. They are in a wide variety of careers. Most of them seem to enjoy a great deal of success and John derives a lot of satisfaction from their success. They have a special spot in his heart and he can remember every player, it seems to me.

"In our travels throughout the U.S., I am always amazed how he is recognized somewhere by someone. It is a rarity for us to spend an evening out without someone stopping John and wanting to talk. This is his most visible side.

"Weekly phone calls keep him in touch with his mother. He is a wonderful son. He is also very good about his relationship with his five sisters and two brothers as well as his uncles and cousins.

"But his greatest joy are his two sons and two daughters. We have a wonderful life together. Our family feels a great closeness."

—Peggy Gagliardi

THE GAG HAS A WAY with his children, too, as Nancy, Gina and John, Jr. find out.

What Gina Gagliardi Says About Gag

"Everything that he touches turns into a golden victory. He's coached football, basketball, baseball, hockey, track and field, and even golf. In John Gagliardi's 37 years of coaching, he has had more winning teams and conference titles than can be imagined. He has also succeeded as an insurance salesman, as a speaker, as an athlete, as a student . . . but very few people know about his greatest success, being a father, husband and friend.

"Dad's 29 years at St. John's haven't been lonely ones. He has good friends helping him through every Saturday of the season. The team doctor, announcer, photographer, chain-gang, scoreboard crew, and "everything man" (Brother Mark) have been with him from the beginning. His wife is his secretary. His one son helps him with coaching and his other son helps with filming. There is nothing fancy about his crew. His devoted fans include coaches, old players and good friends from all over (especially St. Cloud). Those fans rarely miss a game. In fact, St. John's will often bring more fans to away games than the opposing home team.

"Our family can't go anywhere in the U.S. without an old friend recognizing him. Yet, in all this spotlight, Dad still has time for his family. Yes, he is definitely a family man. He seldom goes anywhere without us. Part of his days are spent playing some game with the family.

"When we kids were little, Dad used to play "kick the can" with the whole neighborhood. Our house was like the Kool-Aid commercials, but, Dad was the attraction, not a pitcher of grape Kool-Aid. Now that we're older, the games haven't ended, however they have gotten more challenging.

"Some claim that Dad is blessed with good luck. I don't believe that such an extreme amount of luck exists for one man. Yet, I don't know what it is that makes him succeed in everything. Maybe it's his style, his outlook, his carefree attitude, or his sense of humor, and I guess it is not really worth trying to figure out. We can all just sit back with pride every Saturday of the season and leave all these worries to the third active winningest coach in the entire nation."

—Gina Gagliardi

More Quotes From John

Quarterbacks:

"A quarterback should be able to call his own plays. He's got the feel of the game and he's so much closer to the action."

Missiles:

"Certainly the future of missiles and bombs is important to life. But if you wake up every day worrying about them, you'd never accomplish a thing. I have put my faith in people and God."

Riots:

"The only place I ever want to be in a riot is standing on the corner watching it happen. I hope when anybody mentions hanging me in effigy the students and alumni feel the same way."

Quiet types:

"I love bashful athletes—the kind who'd steal a kiss at an orgy. I find that this kind usually becomes terrible aggressive on the field of strife."

Recruiting:

"Recruiting far and wide may be the answer for the big schools. I just hope at St. John's they come looking for an education first and a pro career second."

Brass:

"At St. John's the administration has been completely fair with me. That's why I don't encourage borderline students to enroll. No talent is worth the embarrassment of failing grades."

Golf:

"I never took the time to learn golf or tennis. I guess you could classify me as a football bum."

Pity:

"I pity young men who are so good in one sport the school won't let them go out for another. Everything in life should be balanced."

Pressure:

"Pressure can kill off so much good, young coaching talent. Most coaches are discouraged before they learn the secrets of the trade."

Posterity:

"When somebody says I have a record that will stand forever, I'm pleased. But I recall the man who asked, 'Why should I worry about posterity—what will it ever do for me?"

Ego:

"The nice thing about football is that it's such a great leveler; it teaches pride—but chastises ego."

Superstions:

"I think superstitions are just the shadows of great truth, as Tyrone Edwards has said. In other words, if we can keep winning in the fourth quarter some sort of superstition has to develop around us."

Winning:

"The only problem with winning a lot is that the loss hurts so much more. But fewer losses hurt less than numerous ones."

Power:

"I see advantages to a mash-mouth power game and also to a hipper-dipper gimmick game. In mash-mouth, the players develop a feeling of physical superiority. In our gimmick-days, we feel more intelligent. The perfect setup, of course, would be a mash-mouth that could be fancy and tricky. That's every coach's dream."

Blue-chippers:

"They talk of skilled blue chippers. We really don't see many at St. John's. What I see is a kid willing to work his tail off to get a great education. That makes him blue chip in my eyes."

Testimonials:

"Testimonials are great for the ego. I just wish my mother could travel with me. She'd believe all the lies."

Mixtures:

"Sometimes at St. John's, I am certain we are affiliated with the equal employment fair practices act. Last year we had a German, Englishman, black and Irishman lined up on one side. If I could have only slipped in a girl."

Confidence:

"I once asked Mike Kozlak how he kept his super attitude while not seeing action as quarterback. He said, 'I have trust and confidence you know what you're doing.' And Paul Schmidt always had a great mental outlook. I remember him saying, 'I just try always to be ready.' Now I sometimes tell my team about these players' attitudes. Having them as a part of the St. John mystique is mighty important."

Followers:

"When I get down after a game I bounce back by realizing that people like Norbert Berg, chairman of the board of Control Data, has followed us closely since attending St. John's. There are many others in that plateau who love the Johnnies dearly and feel we give them something. I can't feel down for long with such quality people enjoying our football."

All-timers:

"When they ask me to name my all-time best players, I refuse. It's the situation that makes the heroes. Some men never get the chance. Others may get many chances."

Tracking:

"I've always felt a team can absorb anything a coach can teach. I get upset when I hear a coach say, 'I don't have a smart team.' He's really admitting he can't get across to them."

Training:

"Nothing is worse in track or horseracing or football than to leave your game on the practice field. Every coach should remember, the game should be fun. Save enough energy for the party."

Roughhousing:

"I've never seen a college team play deliberately dirty football. I've seen some individuals come close. But 'dirty' is a word you can't attribute very often to football. Mr. Cleans outnumber bad boys 100 to one."

Parents:

"I enjoy talking to parents—even the ones who are complainers. The great thing about St. John's, even the complainers are rather impressed with our win record."

Wisdom:

"I've always felt a truly wise man is one who knows his own ignorance. A fool is the man who thinks he knows everything."

Rewards:

"Hearing from a player who starred in football is nice. Hearing from a player who was a fifth-stringer, that's a real reward."

Winning:

"All winning football programs have one thing in common: there are plenty of 'winners' on the team. A winner is not always the fastest, quickest or biggest player on the field. But he is the one that when the game is close will find some way for us to win."

Drugs:

"Drugs and booze in sports? Oh, I suppose it's a problem. But from what I've seen, you have around 10 percent of the average population having trouble with addiction. It's no worse for athletes. They are just ordinary human beings. They have the same problems, pressures, instincts and addictions in proportion to everyone else."

Shakespeare:

"Shakespeare must have been a football fan. When he said 'Cowards die before their death many times' he had to be talking about the poor coaches who give in when they hear the odds. Like Shakespeare, I like to think the valiant die only once."

Passing:

"I am thrilled with a long pass by our team. When the rival throws one, nothing sends shivers down my spine as much."

Bars:

"I never picked up a winning play in a bar."

Johnny tradition:

"I don't say the St. John's athlete is superior to others. But I think the boy who comes here without a scholarship has disciplined his own mind and body to become a success...at whatever he does."

Dates:

"There is one program for my football players I keep promising myself I'll start. That the St. John's grid dating service. I think it would be nice to pair off a senior and frosh and let the senior be responsible to the frosh for getting him acquainted with the girls at St. Benedict's. That freshman year can be awfully lonesome."

Luck:

"It's strange how many players who are called lucky are the ones who keep coming through with big plays consistently. I have to believe the lucky guy in reality is the most coachable, most determined and has the best attitude. If that's luck, order me a shipment by the carload."

Regrets:

"Regrets. Sure. Mostly that I didn't name two or three different captains for each game. That way every young man could have put on his resume that he was a captain at St. John's."

Defense:

"Gee, I can't believe playing defense is that difficult. If the opposition lineman rises up, you know it's a pass. If he goes to his right, you know that's the way the play will probably go. If it's to the left, that's the direction. I may be missing something, but that doesn't seem too difficult."

Trust:

"I consider it an honor when parents turn a young man over to me, entrusting his college future in my hands. It's a very big decision. I hope and pray I'm worthy of the trust."

Film sessions:

"They say I can be a screaming tyrant while looking at our films. Maybe so. But there, in black and white, are the cold facts. No stats, no excuses, no misunderstandings. Facts are facts. And if my team looks bad, somebody has to remind them."

Assistants:

"No, I don't miss not having 12 or 15 assistants. I'd be just worried about stepping on their shoes along the sidelines."

Personal talks:

"Personal confrontations may not be as important as some of the coaches think. A few years ago I urged 50 players through a message to 'talk to me' at any time. I think one or two did—asking me if I knew where they could get a date..."

Recruiting:

"When I recruit for St. John's, I keep hammering at just one fact: The New York Times rating system of colleges put us in the top five in Minnesota and one of the top 250 nationally. That should be a good enough recommendation for any prospect."

Muscles:

"I'm always a little uneasy around young men who can press 400 pounds. I have a feeling that they may be sizing me up for a lofty jerk and that I could be airborne shortly."

Grades:

"I never blame an athlete when he is involved in a grade or scholastic scandal. It is the school that should be scandalized."

Thinking:

"I never want to be like the men who do first, think afterwards and repent forever. I want our team to think coolly, forget the game if we lose and look ahead—not back—the rest of the season."

About Don Riley

A veteran columnist of sports controversy, Don Riley has been a fixture at the *St. Paul Pioneer Press* for 40 years. He has also written three other books — one on the art of selling insurance, another on a notorious safe-cracker and a third on alcoholism. His book, entitled "High and Dry," is used in many schools and was syndicated by *The New York Times.*

Riley has written countless articles for magazines, is quoted in papers from coast to coast and receives, perhaps, more mail than any sports columnist in the country. He has won 18 sportswriting awards, including one in 1984 by the Associated Press for the top column in Minnesota. During his career he has enjoyed conducting sports talk and panel shows on four television stations and six radio stations.

Mr. Riley, who calls college sports his favorite form of competition, has been a long-time admirer of John Gagliardi.

"John coaches football the way presidents should run countries and board chairmen should run corporations," Riley says. "If a player never performs for one minute, he is still getting an education from Gagliardi. John dares to be different. He dares to freshen old concepts and tackle new ones. He is more than a coach; he is a tactician of life, a quality human being of great compassion and integrity."

Mr. Riley lives at home with his wife, Dorothy, in Vadnais Heights, where he is working on a new novel, "Jamestown 101."

He is the father of two grown daughters — Sheila and Shannon.